ARKANSAS
NATIONAL GUARD

WOMEN TRAILBLAZERS

GROUNDBREAKING HISTORY OF THEIR SERVICE IN THE ARKANSAS NATIONAL GUARD

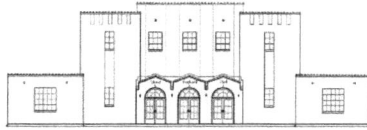

Copyright January 2024
Arkansas National Guard Museum
www.arngmuseum.com

This project was a collaborative effort from the Women's History Committee chaired by BG Leland Tony Shepherd and facilitated by CW3 Darrell Daniels. The committee consisted of retired servicemembers, active servicemembers and the Arkansas National Guard Museum Staff.

ISBN 979-8987527245 – Paperback
ISBN 979-8987527252 – Hardcover

For information about custom editions, special sales, and premium and corporate purchases, please contact the Arkansas National Guard Museum at 501-435-2400 or *arngmuseum@gmail.com.*

This project was funded by the Arkansas National Guard Foundation, which funds programs to preserve the military heritage of the Arkansas National Guard, its units, and its militia predecessors.

Table of Contents

Biographies of the Trailblazers

Valuable Service You Should Know About...
Female Contributions to the Arkansas National Guard

Preface

In this book, you will find historical and present contributions from the women of the Arkansas National Guard and the mountainous value they have given to our organization. Their courage planned and unplanned, conscious, and unconscious has an indelible mark in our history. It is a reminder of their courage, their strength, and their dedication to service. It is also a call to action to ensure that women in Arkansas continue to play a vital role in our organization.

In the Arkansas National Guard, women have served in evolving roles for the past 50 years, even if their contributions have often been overlooked or undervalued. They have climbed to the ranks of General Officer and Command Sergeants Major. They have excelled in such roles as nurses, lawyers, mechanics, finance and accounting, OCS cadre, recruiters, medics, pilots, and engineers. In the past decade they have broken barriers into the combat arms roles of infantry, combat engineer, field artillery and play very important roles in our partnership with SPP Country Guatemala.

Their roles frequently accounted for many "first" female to execute the roles in which they served, making them true pioneers of their gender here in the Great State of Arkansas. They set the standard and bore challenges of being first, but they all conducted themselves

1

with the highest degree of pride and purpose which is the reason we celebrate them in ink. Their stories as you will read are not merely anecdotes, they are testament to courage, leadership, and unwavering commitment to persevere. This gives our organization the strength it needs to be gender diverse and inclusive in breaking down barriers and stereotypes.

These women's stories are enriching and encouraging for all of us and with great admiration from me and the entire organization I would like to extend my thanks to all of them. Their traits will cascade into the current generation of female serving and pave the way for future generation to see what they can be. They led and continue to lead troops with distinction, which we appreciate; thank you for all you've done for us.

BG Leland Tony Shepherd
ATAG - Land Component Commander

History of Women in the Military

For centuries American women have fought for equal participation in the labor force, access to more lucrative positions, financial autonomy, wage equality and more. So, one would likely not expect the Armed Forces to be any different. Women have served their country bravely through multiple wars. But once the fighting ceased, they were expected to step down and return to the norms of typical societal roles in life.

1775-1783 Revolutionary War

During the Revolutionary War, women served the U.S. Army in traditional roles as nurses, seamstresses, and cooks for troops in camp. Though not in uniform, women shared Soldiers' hardships, including inadequate housing and little compensation. Some courageous women served in combat either alongside their husbands or disguised as men, while others operated as spies for the cause. One woman who disguised herself as her husband after his death and took his place firing an artillery piece, is Mary Ludwig Hays also known as Molly Pitcher. The honorable order of Molly Pitcher Award is still awarded to this day. It is awarded to spouses who have voluntarily contributed in a significant way to the improvement of the U.S. Field Artillery or Air Defense Artillery Communities.

1861-1865 Civil War

During the Civil War, women continued to step into many different roles. It was an accepted convention that the Civil War was a man's fight. As with previous wars, publicized images focused on women supporting the war effort as nurses and aides, growing crops, sewing, laundering uniforms and blankets, organizing donations, and serving as romantic spies. This narrative continued to depict women as brave females who maintained the home front in absence of their men. But this picture does not paint the entire story. Although both armies continued to bar the enlistment of women as with the Revolutionary War, women disguised themselves as men and chose to serve. Because they disguised themselves it is impossible to know with any certainty how many female soldiers served during this time.

1917-1918 World War I

In the 20th century things slightly improved for women in the military. Upwards of 25,000 American women between the ages of 21 and 69 served overseas during World War I, primarily as nurses for the Army and switchboard operators for the Army and Navy Signal Corps. Historians believe the service of these women helped propel the passage of the 19th Amendment. On August 26, 1920, the Nineteenth Amendment was officially adopted. This was the culmination of a decades-long movement for women's suffrage at both state and national levels. While women had the right to vote in several of the colonies in what would become the United States, by 1807 women had been denied even limited suffrage. The Equal Rights Amendment (ERA) was introduced in 1923. It provides a fundamental legal remedy against sex discrimination for both women and men. It would guarantee that the rights affirmed by the U.S. Constitution are held equally by all citizens without regard to their gender. It was introduced in Congress for literally 50 years before finally passing and took 97 years to receive ratification in 2020, yet as of April 2023 the amendment is still pending finalization and not a part of the U.S. Constitution.

1939-1945 World War II

Aa a result of unprecedented need for Soldiers, the Army turned to women for help. In efforts to free up men to fight on the front lines, women were recruited to serve in all branches of the military. Three hundred and fifty thousand women served in uniform in WWII. Women served in the following capacities for the Army: The Women's Army Auxiliary Corps (WAACs) reformed to Women's Army Corps (WAC), and Army's Women Airforce Service Pilots (WASPS). The Navy created Women Accepted for Volunteer Emergency Services (WAVES) and the Marine Corps created the Women's Reserve. The Coast Guard established a Women's Reserve (SPARS) or Semper Paraturs, meaning "Always Ready."

1945-1954 Post World War II

Immediately following World War II, women were expected to step down from their role of serving in the U.S. Armed Forces. However, due to the exceptional service of military women during World War II, the Women's Armed Service Integration Act was signed into law by President Harry S. Truman on June 12, 1948. This bill enabled a permanent presence of women in the military, including WAC, WAVE, women in the Marine Corps, and women in the Air Force. It also created for the first time an organized Reserve for each of these branches. The Women's Armed Services Integration Act of 1948 enshrined women's right to serve in the armed forces, they were finally able to serve their country as members of the U.S. Armed Forces during peacetime. However, this legislation also restricted the assignment of women to positions that would not expose them to direct combat and severely restricted their service. It limited the number of women who could serve to 2% of any military branch, allowed the military to involuntarily discharge women who became pregnant, and it limited the number of women who could become officers. The number of women officers could total no more than 10% of the 2%. Promotion of women officers was capped above paygrade 0-3 (Captain/Lieutenant). Paygrade 0-5 (Lieutenant Colonel/Commander) was the highest permanent rank women could obtain. Women serving as directors of Women's Army Corps (WACs), Women Accepted for Voluntary Emergency Services (WAVES), Women in the Air Force (WAFs), and Women Marines could be temporarily promoted to paygrade 0-6 (Colonel/Captain). Most significantly, it prevented women from commanding men or ever serving in combat.

1955-1973 Milestones for Women in the National Guard

In 1956, President Dwight D. Eisenhower signed Public Law No. 845 allowing women to join the National Guard. This law restricted women to serve as officers and only in the medical field. In addition, the number allowed to serve was limited to 2% for each branch. Second Lieutenant Kathleen Booth was the first female to join the Arkansas National Guard when she joined the Air Guard in 1965.

Twelve years later, on November 8, 1967, President Lyndon B. Johnson signed Public Law No. 90-130 which removed the 2% strength and rank ceiling limitations for women. This allowed for assignments outside of the medical field but still restricted from combat arms. Most significantly, women could be promoted to general and flag ranks. The first female generals in U.S. history were nominated for promotion in 1970 by then-president Richard M. Nixon.

As the war in Vietnam ended and the Army began transitioning to an all-volunteer force, the role of women in the Army expanded to help fill vacancies before the draft ended in June 1973. Their success was marked by a request from the Army Chief of Staff to lift the recruitment ceiling on the number of women. In 1971, women with no prior-service experience were permitted to enlist in the National Guard. The Arkansas Air National Guard had its first female enlistment in 1969 and the Arkansas Army National Guard had their first female enlistments in February 1973. It was also during this era that we see the removal of restrictions on promotions, assignments, and utilization.

1974-2010 Military Transformation and Gulf War

The military began a significant transformation period after the Vietnam War. This also mirrored many of the changes going on in society in general. In 1976, for the first-time women were accepted into the military service academies. Throughout the 1970's other barriers dropped, and women were assigned to non-combat naval ships and military aircraft but remained excluded from direct ground combat. During the 1980's the size and capabilities of the U.S. military grew, and women filled more positions. By 1988, the Department of Defense enacted a "risk rule" in an attempt to bar women from non-combat jobs that put them at risk of exposure. However, during the Persian Gulf War the military had over 40,000 women serving in the operation and there was a realization that many of the women were exposed to combat regardless of their direct unit assignment.

This led to legislative changes and in 1993 Congress repealed laws prohibiting women from combat aircraft or naval ships, except submarines. This opened many positions for women in the Air Force and Navy. The Department of Defense was given discretion to determine the limits for women and in 1994 the 'risk rule' was replaced with the Ground Combat Exclusion Policy known as the "Direct Combat Definition and Assignment Rule." This limited women from serving in position at a unit level below brigade size when the primary mission of the unit is direct ground combat. This was not as easily administered as military and civilian leaders had expected. As the US engaged in many operations in the 1990's and early 2000s, there was a growing reality of the inability to remove military women from risk. Additionally, it was apparent that these highly capable women serving in the military were necessary to maintain readiness. During the Persian Gulf War, Operation Iraqi Freedom and Operation Enduring Freedom women serving as military police, truck drivers, helicopter pilots, engineers and many other roles had been at risk, the modern battlefield was not so clearly defined.

7

2013-2016 Women in Combat MOS's

In 2013, Secretary of Defense Leon E. Panetta signed a document to lift the Defense Department's ban on women in direct ground combat roles. This historical decision overturned the 1994 Direct Ground Combat Definition and Assignment Rule that restricted women from Artillery, Armor, Infantry, and other combat roles and military occupational specialties. Just two years later, on December 3, 2015, Secretary of Defense Ash Carter directed the full integration of women in the armed forces following a 30-day review period required by Congress, which was completed April 7. Beginning in January 2016, all military occupations and positions opened to women, without exception. For the first time in U.S. military history, if they qualified and met specific standards, women were able to contribute to the Department of Defense mission with no barriers in their way.

Today, while the overall size of our military remains steady, the percentage of women serving on active duty and in the Reserve component continues to grow in both the enlisted and commissioned ranks, according to the most current released 2021 Demographics Profile of the Military Community.

In 2021, women made up 17.3% of the active-duty force, totaling 231,741 members; and 21.4% of the National Guard and reserves at 171,000 members. The year before, women made up 17.2% of the active-duty force and 21.1% of the Guard and reserve. Since 2017, the percentages of women in the active-duty and selected reserve have risen 1.1% and 1.8% respectively.

Nearly 53 years after initial authorization for female general and flag ranks, in 2020 of the 976 serving generals and admirals in the U.S. military, only 69 were female. To date, there have been 10 four-star General or Admirals in the armed forces. Most recently in 2023, there are four women actively serving at the 4-star rank. They are Admiral Lisa Franchetti, Chief of Naval Operations; Admiral Linda

Fagan, Commandant of the Coast Guard; General Jacqueline Van Ovost, Commander U.S. Transportation Command; and General Laura Richardson, Commander U.S. Southern Command. This demonstrates the slow evolution of change in our Armed Forces and proves that women are more than capable to serve in any position and at all levels when given the opportunity.

Arkansas National Guard

Women have officially served in the U.S. forces for over a century, primarily in the Active component. Unlike the Active U.S. Forces, the history of women serving in the Arkansas National Guard is more recent. Women could not join the Arkansas National Guard until 1956 and they could only join if they were medical officers. The first officer to join was in 1965. The law changed again in 1967 where they were allowed to join as enlisted service members. The first female enlistment was in 1969 and 1973 respectively for the Arkansas Air and Army National Guard, although they were not allowed to serve in combat positions. In the early 2000s, women serving full-time in the Arkansas National Guard, were not allowed to serve in all positions within a combat designated unit. This meant that women who were well qualified in their occupation were skipped over for promotion for a vacancy within specific combat units that had a ground combat exclusion for women. Specifically, the job announcement stated, "This position is closed to females." Today women can hold any position within the Arkansas National Guard. Women faced many issues during the first few decades, but despite these obstacles their contributions to the Air and Army Guard have been momentous. Among the many accomplishments, the Arkansas Air Guard had its first female Brigadier General, the Arkansas Army Guard had a Major General, the State Command Sergeant Major and Command Chief Warrant Officer. And there are many more achievements by women in the Arkansas National Guard, and many more to come. While many glass ceilings have been shattered, others yet remain. Remember when there are no ceilings, the possibilities are unlimited.

References-
Women in the Army | The United States Army
How Women Fought Their Way into the U.S. Armed Forces | HISTORY
Over 200 Years of Service: The History of Women in the U.S. Military · United
Service Organizations (uso.org)

National Archives:
"Women Soldiers of the Civil War" Spring 1993, Vol. 25, No. 1
19th Amendment to the U.S. Constitution: Women's Right to Vote (1920
Congress.gov/19th amendment)

Introduction to the Trailblazer Timeline

The committee realizes this book is a "living document" and is aware that all the accomplishments listed here for the past trailblazers is not fully inclusive of everyone and all accomplishments. The committee was also mindful that as the pioneers moved through the various ranks and positions, that they were often trailblazers for the future servicemembers coming behind them. In many cases, the servicemember's highest rank and/or position is what was documented in this publication with the understanding, that they were also the first in their prior ranks and positions.

As more information is discovered it can be added to the digital format of this book that will reside on the Arkansas National Guard Museum's website. This book is a great framework to document a large majority, and as future women become firsts, names will be added to the timeline, and biographies will be added.

If you have information you'd like to share with the committee, please scan the QR code below and submit your information. Once the information is verified, we will have it added to the digital and/or print version of this book.

Timeline of Women Trailblazers in the Arkansas National Guard

ARMY GUARD

1960s

AIR GUARD

1965
2nd Lt. Kathleen Booth
First Female and First Female Officer 188th Fighter Wing

1969
Lt. Col. Joyce Wilkerson
First Enlisted Female in the Arkansas Air National Guard

1970s

1973
Helen Nichols
First Enlisted Female in the Arkansas Army National Guard

1974
SSG Rebecca W. Amato
First Female Enlisted in HHD, 217th Maintenance Battalion

1974
SFC Virginia Harris
First Female in the 39th Brigade

1976
CSM Deborah J. Collins
First Female United States Property & Fiscal Office in the Internal Review Section

ARMY GUARD	AIR GUARD

ARMY GUARD

1977
CW4 Frances Shaw
First Female to be
Commissioned as a
Warrant Officer

1978
CSM Deborah J. Collins
First Female Instructor NCO
Academy Staff (Regional
Training Institute)

1979
COL Anita E. Deason
First Female Battalion
Administrative Officer in the
Arkansas Army National Guard

1980s

1980
MSG Dorothy R. Hayner
First Female on Title 10 Active
Guard and Reserve Tour

1980
CW4 Dorothy Sealy
First Female Warrant Officer,
39th Infantry Brigade

1981
COL Carol A. Johnson
First Female Detachment
Commander, Headquarters and
Headquarters Company, 39th
Support Battalion

1981
COL Alicia "Cissy" Rucker
First Female in the Arkansas
Army National Guard to Attend
and Graduate the U.S. Army
Rotary Wing School

AIR GUARD

1980
Maj. Gen. Betty L. Mullis
First Female Pilot
Arkansas Air National Guard

1981
Lt. Col. Joyce Wilkerson
First Female Squadron
Commander in the 189th
Tactical Airlift Group (TAG)

ARMY GUARD	AIR GUARD
1982 **COL Alicia "Cissy" Rucker** *First Female Helicopter Pilot*	
1983 **CSM Deborah J. Collins** *First Female President of the Enlisted Association of the Arkansas National Guard*	
1983 **COL Mary Frances "Frankie" Sears** *First Female President of National Guard Association of Arkansas and any National Guard Association in the United States*	
1985 **CW4 Celquetta D. Babb-Pride** *First Female Supervisor Combined Support Maintenance Shop*	
1988 **CSM Jennifer Broach** *First Female Enlisted in the 936th Air Traffic Control Unit*	**1988** **Col. Alice K. Sanders** *First Female Chief of Disaster Preparedness Branch, 189th Mission Support Squadron*
1988 **CSM Deborah J. Collins** *First Female Master Sergeant Deputy Commandant*	
1989 **COL Shirley L. Jones** *First Female Commander of the 125th Medical Battalion (Completed Command in 1989)*	**1989** **Lt. Col. Peggy Frye** *First Female Lieutenant Colonel 188th Fighter Wing*

ARMY GUARD	AIR GUARD

1989
CW2 Edith Milligan
First Female to graduate
from Warrant Officer
Candidate School

1990s

1990
CPT Oneida D. Battle
First Female Equal
Employment Manager
Arkansas Army National Guard

1990
COL Alicia "Cissy" Rucker
First Female State Public
Affairs Officer

1990
COL Mary Frances
"Frankie" Sears
First Arkansas Army National
Guard Female to attend the
U.S. Army War College and
First Army National Guard
Female to Graduate from the
U.S. Army War College

1990
SGT Nancy Stokes
First Female in Kuwait During
the Operation Desert Storm
Ground War

1991
SGT Joann Chasteen
Female Serving the Furthest
into Iraq's Combat Zone
During the Operation Desert
Storm Ground War

1991
Col. Alice K. Sanders
First Female Chief of Supply,
189th Logistics Squadron

15

1991
CSM Deborah J. Collins
First Female to attend the United States Sergeants Major Academy

1991
COL Karen Gattis
First Female Commander, Company D, 114th Air Traffic

1991
MSG Margarett "Margo" Linton
First Female to Receive the Bronze Star

1992
CSM Deborah J. Collins
First Female Command Sergeant Major

1993
CSM Deborah J. Collins
First Female Classification Specialist for the Human Resource Office

1994
MG Patricia Anslow
First Female, Detachment Commander, ISU

1996
LTC Brenda Cluck
First Female Commander Headquarters and Headquarters Battery, 142nd Field Artillery Brigade

1996
CSM Deborah J. Collins
First Female Brigade Operations Sergeant Major for the 87th Troop Command

1994
Brig. Gen. Tamhra L. Hutchins-Frye
First Female Commander 188th Mission Support Flight

1996
CMSgt Donna Lynn Witherow
First Female Chief Master Sergeant 189th Airlift Wing

16

ARMY GUARD	AIR GUARD
1997 **COL Karen Gattis** *First Female Commander,* *172nd Medical Company* *(Air Ambulance)*	**1997** **Col. Alice K. Sanders** *First Female Commander,* *189th Logistics Squadron*
1998 **CSM Deborah J. Collins** *First Female Command* *Sergeant Major for the* *87th Troop Command*	**1998** **CMSgt Brenda L. Aquillino** *First Female Command* *Chief Master Sergeant*
1998 **COL Carol A. Johnson** *First Female Commander,* *212th Signal Battalion*	
1999 **MG Patricia Anslow** *First Female S-3 then XO,* *875th Engineer Battalion* *(Corps Mech)*	**1999** **Capt. Kristin Bass** *First Female Fighter* *Pilot 188th Fighter Wing*
1999 **CSM Gretchen Doty-Evans** *First Female First Sergeant of* *the 239th Military Intelligence* *Company, 39th Infantry Brigade*	
1999 **MAJ Robin Tolliver** *First Winter Biathlon* *Coordinator/Participant* *for Arkansas*	
1999 **SGM Donna Ivey Walker** *First Female Directorate of* *Personnel Sergeant Major*	

17

2000
COL Miriam Carlisle
First Female Senior TAC
Officer Arkansas
Military Academy Officer
Candidate School

2000
CSM Gretchen Doty-Evans
First Female First Sergeant
of 216th MP Company,
87th Troop Command

2001
CSM Jennifer Broach
First Female to accept Title 10
AGR Tour with
NGB Recruiting Team,
Professional Education Center

2001
LTC Brenda Cluck
First Female Aide-de-Camp to
the Arkansas National Guard
Adjutant General

2001
COL Carol A. Johnson
First Female Commander,
87th Troop Command

2002
SGM Deborah
Denise Johnson
First Female Battalion
Operations
Noncommissioned Officer

2002
CW4 Celquetta D.
Babb-Pride
First Female Property Book
Officer for the 233rd Regional
Training Institute

2002
CMSgt Glenda Edwards
First Female Chief Master
Sergeant 188th Fighter Wing

ARMY GUARD	AIR GUARD
2002 **COL Sharon (Sherri) Sims** *First Female Director of the Army National Guard Education Support Center and First in the National Guard to serve as President of the Council of College and Military Educators*	
2003 **LTC Betty Anderson** *First Female Commander to Deploy 216th Military Police Guard Company To Guantanamo Bay, Cuba Arkansas Army National Guard In Support of the Global War on Terrorism*	**2003** **Col. Alice K. Sanders** *First Female Commander, 189th Mission Support Group* **2003** **Col. Alice K. Sanders** *First Female Colonel, 189th Airlift Wing*
2003 **MG Patricia Anslow** *First Female Battalion Commander, 875th Engineer Battalion (Corps Mech) including Operation Iraq Freedom (OIF) 06-08 Deployment*	
2003 **CSM Deborah J. Collins** *First Female State Command Sergeant Major*	
2003 **COL Karen Gattis** *First Female Commander, 1-114th Aviation Battalion*	

19

ARMY GUARD	AIR GUARD
2004 **CW4 Celquetta D. Babb-Pride** *First Female to Serve as Unit Property Book Officer Arkansas Army National Guard* **2005** **SGM Deborah Denise Johnson** *First Female Brigade Full-Time Operations Sergeant Major* **2006** **CSM Jennifer Broach** *First Female First Sergeant Deployed Operation Iraqi Freedom 2006-2007 Company F, 2nd Battalion 211th Aviation Regiment* **2006** **COL Karen Gattis** *First Female Arkansas Army National Guard Pilot to Log Combat Air Mission Hours* **2006** **MAJ Robin Tolliver** *First Female Physician Assistant and Aeronautical Physician Assistant for Arkansas Army National Guard and First Female Troop Medical Clinic Commander* **2007** **COL Karen Gattis** *First Female Commander, 77th Aviation Brigade*	**2007** **Col. Alice K. Sanders** *First Female Vice Commander, 189th Airlift Wing*

ARMY GUARD	AIR GUARD
2008 **CW3 Amelia (Dawson) Penn** *First Female Pilot in Command, Arkansas Army National Guard*	**2008** **Col. Jenny Johnson** *First Female Deputy Staff Judge Advocate, 188th Wing*
2009 **CSM Deborah J. Collins** *First Female Chair Position for the Army National Guard United States Command Sergeant Major Advisory Council*	
2009 **CSM Tammy Treat** *First Female First Sergeant for 119th Mobile Public Affairs Detachment*	

2010s

ARMY GUARD	AIR GUARD
2010 **COL Anita E. Deason** *First Female Human Resources Officer*	**2010** **Lt. Col. Bridgette D. Griffin** *First Female Bronze Star Recipient*
2010 **COL Karen Gattis** *First Female Commander, Marksmanship Training Center*	
2010 **CW5 Pamela Huff** *First Female Chief Warrant Officer Five*	
2011 **COL Miriam Carlisle** *First Female Commander 2nd Battalion, 233rd Regional Training Institute*	

ARMY GUARD	AIR GUARD
2011 **LTC Melissa H. Shipman** *First Female Assault Helicopter* *Company Commander C Co* *1-185th Air Assault*	
2012 **MG Patricia Anslow** *First Female* *Brigadier General,* *Arkansas Army National Guard*	**2012** **Col. Mary Tenise Gardner** *First Female Group* *Commander 188th Wing*
2012 **LTC Natalie Brown** *First Female 39th IBCT* *Brigade Judge Advocate*	
2012 **COL Alicia "Cissy" Rucker** *First Female Inducted into the* *Arkansas Military Academy* *OCS Hall of Fame*	
2012 **LTC Melissa H. Shipman** *First Female Instructor Pilot* *Arkansas Army National Guard*	
2013 **LTC Natalie Brown** *First Female 87th Troop* *Command Brigade* *Judge Advocate*	**2013** **Col. Tina Lipscomb** *First Female Squadron* *Commander 123rd* *Intelligence Squadron*
2013 **CSM Tammy Treat** *First Female Command* *Sergeant Major for 871st* *Troop Command Battalion*	

ARMY GUARD	AIR GUARD

2014
CSM Jennifer Broach
First Female Operations Sergeant Major Recruiting and Retention Command

2014
LTC Natalie Brown
First Female Federal Technician Deputy Staff Judge Advocate

2014
COL Karen Gattis
First Female Director of Joint Staff as a Traditional Soldier

2015
MAJ Clara R. Moser
First Female Field Artillery Officer in the Arkansas Army National Guard

2015
MAJ Clara R. Moser
First Female Company Level Commander of a Field Artillery Firing Battery in the Arkansas Army National Guard

2016
MG Patricia Anslow
First Female Chief of Staff, Kosovo Forces

2016
CSM Jennifer Broach
First Female Command Sergeant Major of Recruiting and Retention Command

---

2014
Col. Sara A. Stigler
First Female Deputy Commander of 188th Wing

2014
Col. Sara A. Stigler
First Commander and Female Commander 153rd Intelligence Squadron

2014
Col. Misty Zelk
First Female Colonel, 188th Wing

2014
Col. Misty Zelk
First Female Medical Group Commander, 188th Wing

2015
Brig. Gen. Bobbi J. Doorenbos
First Female Wing Commander and Air Commander of the 188th Wing

2015
Brig. Gen. Tamhra L. Hutchins-Frye
First Female Full-Time Director Joint Staff Joint Force Headquarters and First Female Brigadier General in the Arkansas Air Guard

ARMY GUARD	AIR GUARD

2016
SPC Shray A. Ricker
First Female in the Arkansas Army National Guard to Graduate From 12B Combat Engineer Reclassification Course

2017
SFC Tasheenia L. Wallace
First Female in the Arkansas Army National Guard to Graduate From the 11B Infantry Transition Course

2017
Col. Jenny Johnson
First Female Executive Officer for the Air National Guard Assistant to the Judge Advocate General of the Air Force

2017
Col. Sara A. Stigler
First Female Commander of 188th Intelligence, Surveillance and Reconnaissance Group

2018
MG Patricia Anslow
First Female Major General, Arkansas National Guard and First Female Chief of Staff, U.S. Southern Command

2018
Col. Sara A. Stigler
First Female Vice Commander of 188th Wing

2018
LTC Natalie Brown
First Female Traditional Arkansas Guardsman Deputy State Judge Advocate

2018
LTC Sharetta Glover
First Female Deputy Commander 61st Civil Support Team

ARMY GUARD	AIR GUARD

2018
LTC Melissa H. Shipman
First Female Brigade Aviation Officer 39th Infantry Brigade Combat Team

2019
MAJ Megan E. Thomas
Frist Female to Graduate from Maneuver Captains Career Course (MCCC), serve as an Infantry Line Company Commander, and Infantry Battalion Operations Officer

2019
SSG Chloe M. Thompson
First Female Enlisted Field Artillery Soldier

2020s

2020
LTC Sandra Y. Young
First Female Commander 217th Brigade Support Battalion 142nd Field Artillery Brigade

2021
MG Patricia Anslow
First Female Deputy Combined Rear Area Coordinator, U.S. Forces Korea

2021
CSM Deborah J. Collins
First Female and First Army Inductee into the Arkansas National Guard Enlisted Hall of Fame

2021
1SG Patricia Halbert
First Female First Sergeant 142nd Brigade Signal Company, 142nd Field Artillery Brigade

ARMY GUARD	AIR GUARD

2021
COL Erica L. Johnson Ingram
First Female Installation Commander Camp J.T. Robinson Maneuver Training Center

2021
1SG Heather L. Peters
First Female First Sergeant of the 106th Army Band

2022
CPT Jamie R. Newton
First Federally Recognized Female Infantry Officer

2022
COL Cory Sailor
First Female Construction & Facility Management Officer (CFMO/DCSEN)

2023
LTC Natalie Brown
First Female Staff Judge Advocate Arkansas National Guard

2023
CW5 Veronica Austin
First Female Command Chief Warrant Officer

2023
CSM Deborah J. Collins
First Female Enlisted Solider to be inducted into the Arkansas Military Veteran's Hall of Fame

2022
Maj. Kimberly M. Hunter
First Female Director of Operations, 188th Intelligence Support Squadron

2022
Col. Sarah O'Banion
First Female Maintenance Group Commander, 189th Airlift Wing

Due to limited access to records, we were not able to find the dates of these trailblazers' accomplishments. However, their achievements are significant and these trailblazers should be recognized.

Lt. Col. Marsha R. Claybrook
First Female Lieutenant Colonel Arkansas Air National Guard

COL Charlotte Yates
First Female Author of the Arkansas Army National Guard Field Sanitation Manual

BIOGRAPHIES OF
ARKANSAS NATIONAL GUARD
WOMEN TRAILBLAZERS

Staff Sergeant Rebecca W. Amato

First Female Enlisted in HHD, 217th Maintenance Battalion

Staff Sergeant (SSG) Rebecca Amato was born January 29, 1939, in Newton County, Arkansas. She graduated from Deer High School in May 1956. She enlisted into the United States Air Force December 16, 1957, as an Airman and served on active duty until December 24, 1959. She married and started a family after her service. She had two years business education at Arkansas Tech University and attended Capital City Business College for one year. On March 23, 1974, she enlisted into the Arkansas Army National Guard, HHD, 217th Maintenance Battalion as a Specialist (E-4), Clerk Typist, MOS 71B10. She was the first female enlistment into the unit. One of her acclaimed accomplishments is that she recruited her niece into the unit. Her niece, CSM Deborah Collins, enlisted on July 30, 1975, during a state-wide recruiting drive with the encouragement of SSG Amato.

On November 7, 1977, SSG Amato transferred to Det 1, 172nd Maintenance Co, into a Fuel & Electrical Systems Repairman with a Military Occupational Specialty (MOS) of 63G20) duty position. She was promoted to Sergeant on May 12, 1978. On February 5, 1981, she again changed duty positions and became the First Cook, MOS 94B30. She was promoted to Staff Sergeant (E-6) on March 13, 1982. On many occasions she accepted Active-Duty Special Work (ADSW) at the NCO Academy, Arkansas Military Academy.

On March 1, 1983, she transferred to 172nd Maintenance Co., Heber Springs as the First Cook. She remained in this duty position until she was reassigned as a Fabric Repairman, MOS 43M10. Due to health issues, she was discharged on October 19, 1989.

After a long courageous battle with cancer, she passed away in July 1995.

Her awards and decorations include the Army Reserve Components Achievement Medal (3), Army Service Ribbon, Army Reserve Components Overseas Training Ribbon, Arkansas Service Ribbon (2) and the ARNG Basic Recruiting Badge.

Lieutenant Colonel
Betty Anderson

First Female Commander to Deploy
216th Military Police Guard Company
to Guantanamo Bay, Cuba
Arkansas Army National Guard
in Support of the Global
War on Terrorism

Lieutenant Colonel (LTC) Betty Anderson was born in Hayti, Missouri. She graduated from South Pemiscot High School located in Steele, Missouri in 1986. In 1990, LTC Anderson received her Bachelor of Arts Degree in Political Science from Murray State University, Murray, Kentucky and in 1993, she received her Master's in Public Administration from Arkansas State University, Jonesboro, Arkansas.

Her military career started on December 31, 1985, when she enlisted in the United States Army Reserve. While attending college at Murray State University, Murray, Kentucky, she joined the Reserve Officer Training Corps (ROTC) Program and received her Commission as a Second Lieutenant in May 1990. After completing the ROTC Program, LTC Anderson was assigned to the United States Army Reserve's 207th Chemical Company in Blytheville, Arkansas.

LTC Anderson began her illustrious military career in the Arkansas Army National Guard on June 1, 1996, with her first assignment as the Rear Area Security Officer at the 25th Rear Tactical Operations Center (RTOC), North Little Rock, Arkansas. She served as Commander of the 216th Military Police Company, West Memphis, Arkansas from 2001-2004. As the Commander of the 216th Military

Police Company, LTC Anderson deployed to Fort Leonard Wood, Missouri in support of "Operation Noble Eagle."

In 2003, the 216th Military Police Guard Company deployed to Guantanamo Bay, Cuba in support of the Global War on Terrorism. LTC Anderson was the first female Commander to deploy the 216th Military Police Guard Company to Guantanamo Bay, Cuba in the history of the Arkansas Army National Guard.

After serving as Company Commander, LTC Anderson served in various other assignments in the Arkansas Army National Guard. In 2004, she was assigned as the Assistant Operations Officer for the 25th RTOC and she served as the Equal Opportunity Advisor for 87th Troop Command from 2006-2009. LTC Anderson served as Adjunct Faculty for Defense Equal Management Institute (DEOMI) from 2008-2011. In 2011, she deployed with the 77th Aviation Brigade as an Equal Opportunity Advisor/Deployable Sexual Assault Response Coordinator in support of Operation Iraqi Freedom Campaign. In 2012, LTC Anderson served as the Provost Marshal for the Institute Support Unit (ISU), Camp J.T. Robinson, Arkansas. She was assigned as a Selective Service Officer for Joint Force Headquarters Arkansas in 2014. In 2015, LTC Anderson was assigned as the Deputy Commander of the Marksmanship Training Unit Brigade Headquarters, Camp J. T. Robinson, Arkansas.

LTC Anderson's military education includes the Military Police Officer Basic Course, Military Police Officer Advance Course, Company/Battery Commanders Course, Corrections Internment and Resettlement Course, Equal Opportunity Reserve Component Course, Equal Opportunity Mediation Course, Combined Arms Exercise Training and the Command and General Staff Officer Course - Intermediate Level Education.

For her outstanding service, she has been awarded the following awards and recognition to include the Meritorious Service Medal, Army Commendation Medal, Army Reserve Achievement Medal,

National Defense Service Medal, Armed Forces Service Medal, Meritorious Unit Commendation, Army Service Ribbon, Parachute Badge, Armed Forces Reserve Medal with "M' Device, Global War on Terrorism Expeditionary Medal, Afghanistan Campaign Medal, Arkansas Service Ribbon, Arkansas Federal Service Ribbon and the Arkansas Emergency Service Ribbon.

LTC Anderson began her civilian career in 1993 as a Human Resources Generalist with the City of Jacksonville, Arkansas. In order to gain experience, she went on to work for several other Government Agencies. From 1995-1997 she worked as an Employment Services Coordinator for Pulaski County Government. In 1997-2001, she began her first Management position for Arkansas Rehabilitation Services as the Assistant Personnel Manager/Grievance Officer.

However, she found her perfect spot with the City of North Little Rock, Arkansas. In 2001, she was hired by former North Little Rock Mayor Patrick H. Hays, as the Equal Opportunity/Fair Housing Director and in 2008; she was promoted to Human Resources Director. LTC Anderson currently works for the City of North Little Rock under Mayor Terry C. Hartwick. She serves as the Human Resources Director, and she also manages the Equal Opportunity Division.

LTC Anderson retired from the military with over 27 years of distinguished service. She currently resides in Maumelle, Arkansas.

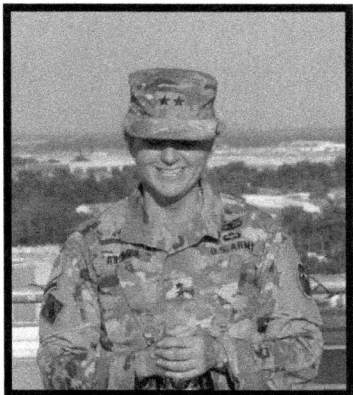

Major General
Patricia M. Anslow

First Female Battalion Commander, 875th Engineer Battalion (Corps Mech) including Operation Iraq Freedom (OIF) 06-08 Deployment

First Female Brigadier General, Arkansas National Guard

First Female Major General, Arkansas National Guard

Major General (MG) Patricia "Trish" Anslow was born in Troy, New York in 1967. In May 1989 she received a Bachelor of Science Degree in Geography and her commission as a Second Lieutenant in the U.S. Army Corps of Engineers from the U.S. Military Academy at West Point, New York. She also received a Bachelor of Science Degree in Biology from the University of Arkansas at Little Rock in 1997, a Master of Science from Johns Hopkins University in 2005 and Masters of Strategic Studies from the US Army War College in 2009.

MG Anslow began her illustrious Army career on active duty. Prior to arriving at her first assignment with the 100th Engineer Company (Topo) in Fort Bragg, North Carolina, she would complete the Engineers Officer Basic Course, the U.S. Army Mapping, Charting and Geodesy Course both at Fort Belvoir, Virginia, and Airborne School at Fort. Benning, Georgia. Several months after arrival and assignment as a platoon leader, in December 1990, the unit arrived in Saudi Arabia in preparation for Desert Shield/Desert Storm. As the Production Platoon leader for the 100th Topographic Engineer Company she was responsible for reproducing all the mapping products for the Central Command (CENTCOM) and Theater

Commander, GEN Schwarzkopf. To say the least, this tough initial assignment prepared her for many future challenges. She served as 100th Engineer Company Executive Officer and 30th Engineer Battalion Personnel Officer (S-1) prior to transitioning to the reserve component in May of 1992.

MG Anslow began her Arkansas Army National Guard career in May 1993 assigned to the Institute Support Unit (ISU) as a traditional member. The majority of her positions in the Arkansas Army National Guard were firsts for females. She became the first female Detachment Commander for the ISU in September 1994. The unit went on to receive the Distinguished Unit Award the following year. She served in staff level positions at Joint Forces Headquarters and 25th Rear Operations Center (ROC) to include a rotation at the Joint Readiness Training Center (JRTC). In 1999, she was assigned as the first female Operations Officer (S-3) of the 875th Engineer Battalion. It was a Corps Mechanized Combat Engineer Battalion and females were restricted from occupying most positions in the Battalion, to include those she was assigned. She went on to serve as the first female Battalion Executive Office and in October 2003 became the first Commander of the Battalion. She commanded the Battalion through their deployment to support Operation Iraqi Freedom (O6-08). The 875th Engineer Battalion transitioned to a route clearance mission and integrated various Active, Reserve Component and National Guard units into the Battalion throughout the deployment. The unit increased in size when their mission changed to support the 3rd ID during the surge operations. The unit was equally proud of receiving the 2007 Walter T. Kerwin Award by the Association of the United States Army (AUSA) for the top unit in the Army for readiness and training. MG Anslow also served as 87th Troop Command Commander and first female Deputy Chief of Staff for Engineering at the State Headquarters prior to her promotion to Brigadier General. In July 2012, she became the first female promoted to Brigadier General in the Arkansas National Guard. She served as first female Joint Forces Headquarters Commander and in October 2013 became the first female Army Commander (Land Component Commander) for the Arkansas Army National Guard. She also achieved many firsts for females in positions outside the state. She was dual hatted in March 2014 as the Deputy Commanding General (DCG), 1st Army Division East, to our knowledge the first female to serve in the position. In June 2016, she deployed to Pristina, Kosovo and served as the first female Chief of Staff for the NATO Kosovo Forces (KFOR) comprising 29 separate nations. This was also a joint assignment opening up more opportunities. In September 2017, following the deployment she began an assignment as a special assistant to the Deputy Chief National Guard Bureau (NGB) supporting response efforts to Hurricane Harvey, Irma, and Maria. She later served as the Deputy Commanding General, Operations for U.S. Army South in San Antonio, Texas. In July 2018, she was the first female in the Arkansas National Guard promoted to Major General. She became the first female assigned to the Title 10 position of Chief of Staff, U.S. Southern Command. In February 2021, she was the first female assigned as the Deputy Combined Rear Area Commander (DCRAC) in U.S. Forces Korea.

MG Anslow served in 5 of the 6 geographic combatant commands throughout her career with the Army National Guard. She supported military humanitarian responses in Guatemala and New Orleans. She also had the unique opportunity to serve in all the mission areas of the U.S. Army Corps of Engineers in and out of uniform - topographic, combat, facilities, construction, and civil works engineering.

Her military education includes numerous courses; some highlights include resident U.S. Army War College, NORTHCOM Dual Status Commanders Course and Certification, NATO Defense College Generals, Flag Officers, and Ambassador Course; Harvard University, Senior Executives in National & International Security Course, and DOD CAPSTONE.

MG Anslow's career was marked with distinction through the receipt of the many awards, decorations, and honors. A few of the highlights are the Defense Superior Service Medal, Legion of Merit Medal, Bronze Star, Humanitarian Service Medal, NATO Medal Non-Article 5 (Balkans), Korea Service Medal, Southwest Asia Service Medal, Kuwait Liberation Medal (Saudi Arabia and Kuwait), Joint Meritorious Unit Citation, Meritorious Unit Citation, Combat Action Badge, and Arkansas Distinguished Service Ribbon. Other honors she has received include the Silver level of the De Fleury Medal, the Hungarian Service Medal of Merit in Gold Grade, Polish Army Medal in Bronze Grade, and the Italian Service Medal.

MG Anslow retired from the Army on July 31, 2022, with over 33 years of military service and retired on October 31, 2023, from the U.S. Army Corps of Engineers with more than 36 years of federal civilian service. Major General Anslow and her spouse COL Gattis are both retired and reside in Fayetteville, Arkansas with their two dogs Roxie and Cali.

Command Chief Master Sergeant
Brenda L. Aquillino

First Female Command
Chief Master Sergeant
Arkansas Air National Guard

Chief Master Sergeant (CMSgt) Brenda L. Aquilino was born August 1940, in Dunsmuir, California. She attended elementary school at Gilchrist, Oregon and Grapevine, Arkansas. Brenda attended high school in Mojave, California and graduated High School in Sheridan Arkansas, May 1958.

CMSgt Aquilino enlisted in the United States Air Force (USAF) on October 22, 1958. She was assigned as an Administration Specialist to 814th Combat Support Group (SAC), Westover AFB, Massachusetts. On January 21, 1960, she received an Honorable Discharge due to the fact she had married and became pregnant. During this time, the military did not allow females to stay in the service if pregnant, so CCM Aquilino had a 15-year break in service.

CMSgt Aquilino re-enlisted in January 1975 as an Administration Specialist (E-4) with the United Coast Guard at Sandy Hook, New Jersey. In November 1977, she transferred to the Arkansas Air National Guard at Little Rock AFB, where she was assigned as Photo Processing Specialist (E-5) with the 123rd Reconnaissance Technical Squadron. She was recognized as The Adjutant General's NCO of the Year 1992 for Arkansas. In 1992, she transferred as NCOIC (E-7) of 189th Training Squadron. In July 1995, she was appointed to Superintendent (E-8) of 189th Services Squadron. In 1997, she was assigned to Headquarters Air National Guard as Visual Information Superintendent (E-9).

CMSgt Aquilino became the first female to hold the position of Command Chief Master Sergeant for the Arkansas Air National Guard in July 1998. She held this position until she retired on August 19, 2000.

CMSgt Aquilino's awards and decorations included the Meritorious Service Medal; Air Force Commendation Medal; Air Force Achievement Medal; NCO Professional Military Education Ribbon with 2 devices; Air Reserve Forces Meritorious Service Medal with 4 devices; Air Force Longevity Service Award with 4 devices; National Defense Service Medal; Air Force Training Ribbon; Armed Forces Reserve Medal; Arkansas Service Ribbon with 2 devices.

After retirement CMSgt Aquilino's received her degree of Bachelor of Science from John Brown University in Siloam Springs, Arkansas on December 16, 2000. She received her degree of Master of Business Administration degree from Webster University George Herbert Walker School of Business & Technology on December 18, 2004. She continues to be an active life member in the Enlisted Association Arkansas National Guard; the Enlisted Association of the National Guard of the United States; And the NCO Academy Graduate's Association. CMSgt Aquilino is married to Frank Rapolla, and they reside in Cape Coral, Florida and are active members of Cape Christian Church.

Chief Warrant Officer Five
Veronica Austin

First Female
Command Chief Warrant Officer
Arkansas Army National Guard

Chief Warrant Officer Five (CW5) Veronica Austin was born in Little Rock, Arkansas. She attended Parkview High School and graduated in May 1985. She received her Bachelor of Business Administration in Computer Information Systems from the University of Little Rock at Little Rock in December 2003.

Her military career started in 1986 when she joined the 25th Rear Area Operations Center, Arkansas Army National Guard as a Private First Class (E3). She completed her Basic Combat Training at Fort Dix, New Jersey and her Advance Individual Training at Fort Benjamin Harrison, Indiana where she acquired the Military Occupational Skill 75B10, Personnel Administration Specialist. She was later promoted to Specialist (E4) in 1988. In 1991, CW5 Austin deployed with the 25th Rear Area Operations Center in support of Operations Desert Storm.

At the beginning of her military career, CW5 Austin worked on active-duty orders from 1988-1989 for the National Guard Bureau Professional Education Center, Camp J.T. Robinson, North Little Rock, Arkansas. In 1990, CW5 Austin was hired in the Federal Military Technician Program as a GS-5 Secretary at the Directorate of Logistics, Arkansas Army National Guard. She worked in the Directorate of Logistics for 9 years.

In 1998 CW5 Austin attended Warrant Officer Candidate School, at Fort Rucker, Alabama, where she was the honor graduate. On September 26, 1999, CW5 Austin received her commission as

Warrant Officer One (WO1), 420A, Military Personnel Technician and was promoted to the grade of GS-10. She was assigned as the Human Resources Specialist for the Institute Training Unit, Camp J.T. Robinson. CW5 Austin was later promoted to GS-11 and assigned to the 35th Aviation Brigade, Camp J.T. Robinson, where she served as the S1 Personnel Officer. Additionally, CW5 Austin was assigned to the Deputy Chief of Staff Personnel as the SIDPERS Chief. She served in the Federal Military Technician Program for 20 years.

In 2010, CW5 Austin was hired into the Title 10 Active Guard Reserve (AGR) Program at the Human Resources Training Center, National Guard Professional Education Center, where she served as the Senior Instructor. In 2013, CW5 Austin was hired into the Title 32 Active Guard Reserve (AGR) Program for Arkansas Army National Guard as the Administrative Officer for Joint Force Headquarters, Camp J.T. Robinson. While a member of the Title 32 AGR Program, she has served in a variety of positions to include Officer Personnel Manager at Deputy Chief of Staff Personnel and State Equal Employment Manager (SEEM), Human Resources Office. In May of 2023, CW5 Austin was promoted to Chief Warrant Officer Five (CW5) and was reassigned to the Deputy Chief of Staff Personnel as the Officer Personnel Manager. On August 22, 2023, CW5 Austin was selected as the 8th Command Chief Warrant Officer of Arkansas Army National Guard. She is the first female in the history of the Arkansas National Guard that has been selected as the Command Chief Warrant Officer.

CW5 Austin's military education includes the Warrant Officer Candidate School, Warrant Officer Staff Course Phase II, Officer in Charge Course, Composite Risk Management Basic Course, Administrative Officer Workshop, Physical Security Inspectors Course, Homeland Security Liaison Officer Program, Warrant Officer Senior Service Education, and the United States Military Entrance Processing Command (USMEPCOM) Antiterrorism Level 1 Course.

Her awards and decorations include the Meritorious Service Medal, Army Commendation Medal, Army Achievement Medal, Army Reserve Component Achievement Medal, National Defense Service Medal, Kuwait Liberation Medal, Kuwait Liberation Medal (Saudi Arabia), Noncommissioned Officer Professional Development Ribbon, Army Service Ribbon, Southwest Asia Service Medal, Army Reserve Overseas Training Ribbon, Armed Forces Reserve Medal with "M" device, Arkansas Emergency Service Medal, Arkansas Federal Service Ribbon, and the Arkansas Service Ribbon.

CW5 Austin currently resides in Sherwood, Arkansas. She has one son, Malique and a grandson Malique Jr.

Chief Warrant Officer Four
Celquetta D. Babb-Pride

First Female Supervisor
Combined Support Maintenance Shop

First Female to Serve as Unit Property
Book Officer
Arkansas Army National Guard

Chief Warrant Officer Four (CW4) Celquetta Pride was born in Malvern, Arkansas. She graduated from Mountain Pine High School in 1979. CW4 Pride received an Associate Degree of Science from Vincennes University and a Bachelor of Science in Leadership and Ministry from Central Baptist College.

CW4 Pride military career started in the United States Army on July 2, 1979. She completed Basic Combat Training at Fort Dix, New Jersey. She received her Advanced Individual Training (AIT) at Fort Lee, Virginia, where she acquired the Military Occupational Skill of 76C10, Equipment Records and Parts Specialist. Her first assignment was with the 227th Aviation Battalion at Fort Hood, Texas. She was honorably discharged from the U.S. Army in July 1982.

In September 1982, CW4 Pride enlisted into the Arkansas Army National Guard and was assigned to several units, the 212th Signal Battalion, Detachment 1, Company B, 935th Aviation Support Battalion, and Company C, 38th Aviation Battalion. Her duty assignments consisted of Equipment Records and Parts Specialist (76C), Automated Logistical Specialist and Unit Supply Clerk (92Y30).

In April 1984, CW4 Pride was hired into the Full-Time Federal Technician Program at the Arkansas Army National Guard Combined Support Maintenance Shop (CSMS), Camp J.T. Robinson. During her tenure at CSMS, she worked in various positions such as a Surface

Maintenance Dispatcher (GS-4), Supply Clerk (GS-6), Tools and Parts Attendant Supervisor (WG-4) and as a Senior Production Controller (GS-8). The highest position that CW4 Pride obtained in the Federal Technician Program was the GS-9, Equipment Specialist position in Deputy Chief of Staff, Logistic (DCSLOG), Camp J.T. Robinson.

In 1985, CW4 Pride was the first female Supervisor assigned to the Arkansas Army National Guard Combined Support Maintenance Shop and the first female to serve as an Equipment Specialist for DCSLOG.

On August 28, 2002, CW4 Pride received her commission as a Warrant Officer and her duty assignment was with Headquarters and Headquarters Company, 233rd Regiment Regional Training Institute at Camp J.T. Robinson as the Property Book Officer. CW4 Pride was the first female assigned to the Property Book Officer's position. Subsequent to the Property Book position, CW4 Pride retired from the Federal Technician Program with 20 years of Federal Service.

In May 2004, CW4 Pride was hired into the Active Guard Reserve (AGR) Program as a Property Book Officer (PBO) for HHC, 212th Signal Battalion, Arkansas Army National Guard. She was the first female to serve as PBO in the 212th Signal Battalion. In 2006, she was assigned to the 39th Infantry Brigade Combat Team as the Brigade's Property Book Officer. CW4 Pride was the first female to serve as the Property Book Officer for the 39th IBCT. The 39th IBCT is the largest Brigade in the Arkansas Army National Guard with approximately 4,000 soldiers assigned.

In 2009, CW4 Pride served as Property Book Officer for the 777th Aviation Support Battalion, 77th Aviation Brigade, Camp Robinson. She was the first female to serve as the Property Book Officer in the 77th Aviation Brigade. In August 2013, she was assigned to Joint Force Headquarter-Arkansas, DSLOG, Camp Robinson. Upon Brigade's request, in August 2016, CW4 Pride was assigned to the 77th Aviation Brigade, Arkansas Army National Guard to serve as Property Book Officer. After completing her assignment with the 77th Aviation

Brigade, CW4 Pride was reassigned to Joint Force Headquarter in 2019.

CW4 Pride's military education includes 76C, Equipment Records and Parts Specialist, AIT, National Guard Battle Skills Course, Basic Noncommissioned Officer Course, Warrant Officer Candidate Course, Warrant Officer Basic Course, Warrant Officer Advanced Course, Warrant Officer Staff Course, Property Accounting Technician Warrant Officer Advance Course, Material Control/Accounting Specialist Course, Standard Property Book System Course, Basic Property Accounting/PBUSE GGSS-Army Property Book Course, Supply Manager Course, Unit Supply Specialist Basic Technical Course, Unit Supply Enhancing Course, Surface Maintenance Management Support Course, SAMS-1 Course, OMS/UTES Supply Technician Course, Supervisory Personnel Management Office Course, Supervisor Personnel Management Office Supervisor Training Course, and the Food Operations Management Course.

CW4 Pride's military awards and citations include the Army Commendation Medal (2nd Award), Army Achievement Medal (2nd Award), Army Good Conduct Medal, Army Reserve Component Achievement Medal (8th Award), National Defense Service Medal w/ Bronze Service Star, Global War On Terrorism Service Medal, Noncommissioned Officer Professional Development Ribbon (2nd Award), Army Service Ribbon, Army Component Overseas Training Ribbon, Armed Forces Reserve Medal (3rd Award), Department of the Army Certificate Of Achievement, Certificate of Achievement, United States Army Quartermaster School Noncommissioned Officer Academy, 1st Cavalry Division Certificate of Achievement, Letter of Commendation's (3), and Letter of Appreciation (2).

CW4 Pride served as past board member for National Guard Association of Arkansas (NGAA), and she volunteers to read for Literacy Program at local schools. She enjoys traveling and spending time with her daughter and other family members. She is currently active in her church and serves as Treasurer for Grace National Apostolic Fellowship and Assembly of Churches.

CW4 Pride is very thankful to all the Pioneers that came before her and everyone that believed in her. She's most of all grateful to God. CW4 Celquetta Pride retired in August 2019 after over 40 years of distinguished military service.

Captain Kristin Bass

First Female Fighter Pilot
188th Wing,
Arkansas Air National Guard

Captain (Capt.) Kristin L. Bass was raised in Colorado and graduated from Oklahoma State University. In 1999, at the age of 23, she began the journey to become an F-16 pilot. When she was a Second Lieutenant, Capt. Bass was accepted into the188th Fighter Wing's Pilot Trainee Program.

In February 1999, Capt. Bass made history by becoming the first female fighter pilot assigned at the 188th Fighter Wing, Arkansas Air National Guard, Fort Smith. Capt. Bass flew both F-16 Fighting Falcons and A-10C Thunderbolt II "Warthogs" during her stint at 188th. She made her first training mission flight with F-16 Fighting Falcon on April 4, 2002, and later she became an A-10 Thunderbolt II "Warthogs" pilot until 2008, following her final flight with A-10 at the 188th Fighter Wing in Fort Smith, October 6, 2008.

She has been announced in Air Force news and media several times, as one of the first women fighter pilots who earned respect on Air Force magazine article "The Quiet Pioneers" in December 2002. On March 6, 2010, the 188th Fighter Wing's celebration for Women's History Month honored her achievements. Flying Razorback Flashback acknowledged her as 188th's first female pilot in March 2015, and she was featured in *Women at War: Iraq, Afghanistan, and Other Conflicts*, a book written by James E. Wise, Jr., Scott Baron, Naval Institute Press, 2011.

Captain Oneida D. Battle

First Female Equal Employment Manager
Arkansas Army National Guard

Captain (CPT) Oneida D. Battle was born in Landstuhl, Germany. She graduated from Henry Foss Senior High School in 1977. CPT Battle graduated Summa Cum Laude from the Pacific Lutheran University obtaining her Bachelor of Arts in Political Science on May 23, 1982. She received a Master of Arts Degree from Pacific Lutheran University on August 23, 1991.

CPT Battle began her military career on February 13, 1981, when she enlisted in the Washington Army National Guard in Tacoma, as a Still Photo Specialist (84B10) as part of the Split Option Training Program. During the same period, she completed Basic Training and Advanced Individual Training and was awarded the Nuclear Biological and Chemical (NBC) Military Occupational Specialty (54E). In June 1983, CPT Battle attended Officer Candidate School (OCS) at the Washington Military Academy. On July 21, 1984, she completed the OCS Program and was commissioned as 2nd Lieutenant Transportation Officer Branch.

After receiving her commission, CPT Battle served as the Chemical, Biological and Radiological (CBR) Team Chief in the 116th Rear Area Operation Center (RAOC) at Camp Murray, Tacoma. During this assignment, she performed temporary duty in Brussels, Belgium. On May 12, 1987, CPT Battle was assigned as Platoon Leader, 1161st Transportation Company, Ephrata, Washington. That was a short-lived assignment and in July of the same year she was transferred to Headquarters and Headquarters Detachment (HHD), 248th Transportation Battalion in Montesano, Washington. She served as Detachment Commander for nearly two years. In January

1989, she assumed the role of Executive Officer for the 541st Personnel Services Company at Camp Murray in Tacoma. On December 3, 1990, CPT Battle transferred from the Washington Army National Guard to the Arkansas Army National Guard and was hired as the first female Equal Employment Manager in the history of the Arkansas National Guard.

CPT Battle served with distinction in her role as State Equal Employment Manager. She was awarded a Memorandum of Appreciation from the Chief, Equal Opportunity Division, National Guard Bureau (NGB) for her participation in the second workshop of its kind focusing on equal opportunity challenges and opportunities in the National Guard. On August 31, 1994, CPT Battle transferred from the Arkansas Army National Guard to the Arkansas Air National Guard and was assigned to the 189th Mission Support Squadron, 189th Airlift Wing, Jacksonville.

CPT Battle's profession military education include the Transportation Officer Basic Course, Transportation Officer Advanced Course, the Department of Defense (DOD) Defense Equal Opportunity Management Institute, Patrick Air Force Base Phase 1-III course for Equal Opportunity Advisors and Equal Opportunity Representative Course.

CPT Battle's service was recognized for its excellence through the receipt of the following awards, decorations, and honors to include the Army Commendation Medal, Army Achievement Medal, Army Reserve Components Achievement Medal, National Defense Medal, Army Service Ribbon, Army Reserve Component Training Ribbon, and Arkansas Commendation Medal.

Second Lieutenant
Kathleen Booth

First Female and First Female
Officer in the 188th Fighter Wing,
Arkansas Air National Guard

Second Lieutenant (2nd Lt.) Booth was originally from Cedar Rapids, Iowa and moved to Fort Smith, Arkansas in 1960 to attend the Sparks Hospital School of Nursing.

On July 18, 1965, 2nd Lt. Booth was commissioned as the unit's only nurse at the time. Booth worked in the unit's dispensary and in her civilian career she was a registered nurse at the Fort Smith Health Center. When 2nd Lt. Booth commissioned, she became the first female member and first female Officer at the 188th Tactical Reconnaissance Group in Fort Smith.

Command Sergeant Major Jennifer Broach

First Female Enlisted in the 936th Air Traffic Control Unit

First Female First Sergeant Deployed Operation Iraqi Freedom 2006-2007 Company F, 2nd Battalion 211th Aviation Regiment

First Female Command Sergeant Major of Recruiting and Retention Command

Command Sergeant Major (CSM) Jennifer Broach was born and raised in North Little Rock, Arkansas. She attended Catholic schools from first grade through twelfth grade, where she graduated from Mount St. Mary Academy in Little Rock, Arkansas in 1985. She enrolled in college for one semester at the University of Central Arkansas in Conway. After her departure from there, she found employment at Cajun's Wharf in Little Rock, Arkansas and became friends with a strong military family. Albert Jr. and Kirk Van Pelt, both convinced her to join the Arkansas National Guard at the age of twenty-one.

CSM Broach's career includes many firsts, this pushed her to achieve her goals. Her first love is Army Aviation and will always be her military family.

On October 27, 1988, CSM Broach enlisted in the 936th Air Traffic Control (ATC) where she was the only female in the unit. She served in the unit until October 1, 1994, when she was assigned to the USAR Control Group. On July 1, 1997, CSM Broach returned to the Arkansas National Guard. She was assigned to 2nd BN 233rd Regional Training Institute as a Training Sergeant. On October 1, 1999, CSM Broach accepted a full-time Recruiting and Retention NCO position and was the only female full-time Recruiter. On December 1, 2001, CSM Broach accepted a Title 10 AGR Tour with National Guard Bureau Recruiting Team at the Professional Education Center. Again, she was the only female on the team and was selected as Instructor of the Quarter in 2002. CSM Broach returned to the Arkansas Recruiting and Retention Force on September 1, 2003.

Then on December 1, 2003, CSM Broach was assigned to HHD 2nd 114th Air Traffic Controllers and was deployed for Operation Iraqi Freedom (OIF) deployment in 2003-2004. Upon return from her deployment, she was reassigned back to the Recruiting and Retention Command and served there until March 1, 2006, when once again she was deployed for OIF 2006-2007 as the First Sergeant of Co F, 2nd Bn 211th Aviation Regiment. She was the first female 1SG to deploy in OIF. On October 1, 2008, CSM Broach was reassigned to Joint Force Headquarter to serve as the Executive NCO for the State Command Sergeant Major. She served in the position until April 2, 2012, when she was reassigned as the Human Resources NCO at the 77th Aviation Brigide. On January 20, 2014, CSM Broach was reassigned as an AREA NCOIC in Recruiting and Retention Command, again a first. On March 17, 2015, CSM Broach was promoted to SGM and became the first female RRC Operations SGM. Then on September 29, 2016, she was laterally appointed to Command Sergeant Major and became the first female CSM for the RRC and the fourth female CSM in the state. On April 19, 2018, CSM Broach returned to aviation and became the Aviation Operations Chief.

On November 1, 2018, CSM Broach retired from service. She spent close to thirty years serving her state and nation and retired to continue the tradition of leadership by becoming an Army Instructor at Conway High School Junior Reserve Officer Training Corps program, where she continues to serve.

Sergeant Major Broach is married to Bill Broach, they live in Conway, Arkansas where she enjoys golf and her family. Her son

William, her pups, Adah, and Boo, and meeting new friends on the golf course.

A quote she shared here to highlight her motivation.

> *Men were told they are supposed to be leaders, while women were told they were not strong enough to be leaders. There is one crucial factor missing in this. The more a woman is told,' No you cannot, or you are not supposed to...,' the more she pushes to prove them wrong. For women, accomplishing leadership is not a "given" rite of passage, but one which is "earned." And that is something she will never forget. Stay true to your faith, be a good and positive person, and encourage others along your way to destiny. And never, ever give up on yourself or your dreams!*

Lieutenant Colonel
Natalie Brown

First Female 39th IBCT Brigade Judge Advocate

First Female 87th Troop Command Brigade Judge Advocate

First Female Staff Judge Advocate Arkansas National Guard

Lieutenant Colonel (LTC) Natalie Garland Brown was born in Jonesboro, Arkansas. She graduated from Westside High School in 2001. LTC Brown graduated with a Bachelor of Arts Degree in History from Arkansas State University in 2005. She obtained her Juris Doctorate from the University of Arkansas at Little Rock William H. Bowen School of Law in 2008.

LTC Brown began her military career by enlisting in the Arkansas Army National Guard on February 16, 2006, as a Unit Supply Specialist in the 875th Engineer Battalion, 87th Troop Command. In February 2010, she commissioned as a First Lieutenant in the Judge Advocate General's Corps.

LTC Brown completed the Judge Advocate Officer Basic Course in 2010 and was assigned to Joint Force Headquarters as a defense counsel for the Arkansas Army National Guard. She completed the Judge Advocate Officer Advanced Course in January 2014, the Intermediate Level Education Course in August 2017, and the Advanced Operations Course in May 2019.

LTC Brown has served in a variety of assignments as a Judge Advocate. As a traditional Arkansas National Guardsman, she has served as a trial defense counsel for the Arkansas Army National Guard from 2010 to 2012. She was appointed as the 39th IBCT

Brigade Judge Advocate in June 2012. In November 2013, she was appointed 87th Troop Command Brigade Judge Advocate. She returned to the 39th IBCT as the Brigade Judge Advocate in February 2016. Her current role as a traditional Arkansas Guardsman is as the Deputy State Judge Advocate, a position she was appointed to in July 2018. In each of these roles, she has been the first female Judge Advocate assigned for the Arkansas National Guard. Additional assignments LTC Brown has held for the Arkansas National Guard include State Ethics Counselor, Chief of Administrative Law, Chief of Legal Assistance, and Chief of Operational Law.

LTC Brown serves the Arkansas National Guard as a federal technician. In 2014, LTC Brown was hired as the Deputy Staff Judge Advocate for the Arkansas National Guard. Prior to this position, she was the State Attorney for the Arkansas Military Department from 2010 to 2014. LTC Brown was appointed as the Staff Judge Advocate for the Arkansas National Guard in January 2023. As the Staff Judge Advocate, LTC Brown is the primary legal advisor to The Adjutant General, the Arkansas National Guard Command Team, Staff, and Directorates. She is the first female Staff Judge Advocate of the Arkansas National Guard.

LTC Brown is a lifetime member of the National Guard Association of Arkansas and National Guard Association of the United States.

LTC Brown's awards and decorations include the Meritorious Service Medal with two Bronze Oak Leaf Clusters, Army Commendation Medal with two Bronze Oak Leaf Clusters, Army Achievement Medal with two Bronze Oak Leaf Clusters, Army Reserve Component Achievement Medal with four Bronze Oak Leaf Clusters, Arkansas Distinguished Service Medal, Arkansas Exceptional Service Medal, the Arkansas Recruiting Ribbon, and the Arkansas Service Ribbon with two Diamond Devices.

Colonel Miriam Carlisle

First Female Senior TAC Officer Arkansas Military Academy Officer Candidate School

First Female Commander 2nd Battalion, 233rd Regional Training Institute Arkansas Army National Guard

Colonel (COL) Miriam Carlisle was born in Galveston, Texas. In 1989 she graduated from Hendrix College in Conway, Arkansas with a Bachelor's Degree in Psychology. She graduated from Webster University with a Master's Degree in Management and Leadership in 2015.

COL Carlisle began her military career in January 1991, by enlisting in the Arkansas Army National Guard's 936th Air Traffic Control Platoon. In June 1993, she was commissioned through the Arkansas Military Academy Officer Candidate School as a Second Lieutenant in the Signal Corps and was assigned to the 212th Signal Battalion. She served 28 years in the Arkansas National Guard, before transferring to the United States Army Reserve in March 2019.

While serving in the Arkansas Army National Guard, COL Carlisle served in various command and leadership positions including Platoon Leader, Executive Officer, and Company Commander in the 212th Signal Battalion. She served in the 233rd Regional Training Institute (RTI) as a TAC (Teach, Advise, Counsel) Officer and in 2000, she was assigned as the Senior TAC Officer for the Officer Candidate School. COL Carlisle was the first female to serve as the Senior TAC Officer in the history of the Arkansas Military Academy's Officer

Candidate School. COL Carlisle was assigned to the Joint Force Headquarters Arkansas (JFHQ-AR) G3 as the Force Integration and Readiness Officer, and later as the Executive Officer for the Arkansas National Guard Land Component Commander. In 2011, she assumed command of 2nd Battalion, 233rd Regional Training Institute and became the first female Commander of the 2nd Battalion, 233rd Regiment, Arkansas Army National Guard. COL Carlisle served in the JFHQ-AR G4 office as the Property Book Officer for the state's nine maintenance shops, and then in the JFHQ-AR G1 as the State Family Program Director.

Because of her former police officer experience, she was assigned as the Arkansas National Guard's Force Protection/Antiterrorism Officer in the JFHQ-AR J3/DOMS. She mobilized in support of NATO's multi-national, Kosovo Forces (KFOR) mission in Kosovo where she served as the U.S. Military Assistant to the Italian Major General KFOR Commander. After her deployment, she was assigned to the JFHQ-AR G4 office as the current Operations Chief for Logistics.

COL Carlisle transferred to the United States Army Reserve where she was hired as the Deputy Chief of Staff, G4 with the 412th Theater Engineer Command, Vicksburg, Mississippi and finally as the Assistant Chief of Staff G4 with the 84th Training Command, Fort Knox, Kentucky.

COL Carlisle's military education includes the Signal Officer Basic Course, Signal Officer Advance Course; Adjutant General Officer Advance Course; Senior Transportation Officer Qualification Course; Theater Sustainment Command Qualification Course; Command and General Staff Course (ILE); the Advanced Operations Warfighting Course, Support Operations Course, Advanced Property Management Course, Strategic Planning and Management Course, Antiterrorism Basic Course, Operations Security Level II Course and the Department of Defense Assurance Assessment Course.

During her outstanding military career, she has received numerous awards and decorations including the Defense Meritorious Service Medal, the Meritorious Service Medal, the Army Commendation Medal, the Army Achievement Medal, the Army Reserve Components Achievement Medal, the National Defense Service Medal, the Armed Forces Expeditionary Medal, the Korea Defense Service Medal, the Armed Forces Service Medal, the Armed Forces Reserve Medal, the Army Overseas Ribbon, the Army Reserve Components Overseas Training Ribbon, NATO Non-Article 5 for the Balkans, and the Italian Commemorative Cross for the Peacekeeping Mission in Kosovo. She was also awarded the Bronze Order of Mercury and the Distinguished Order of Saint Martin.

COL Carlisle retired as the Assistant Chief of Staff (ACoS) G4 for the 84th Training Command in Fort Knox, Kentucky on July 1, 2023, with over 32 years of distinguished military service. She resides in Sherwood, Arkansas along with her husband Joseph Westfall and daughter Lauren.

SGT Jo Ann Chasteen

Female Serving the Furthest into Iraq's Combat Zone During the Operation Desert Storm Ground War

SGT Chasteen served with Arkansas Army National Guard 25th Rear Area Operations Center (RAOC) during Operation Desert Storm. She was attached to the G-3 Section of the 18th Airborne Corp and accompanied them to Iraq. In 1991, SGT Chasteen went further into Iraq than any other female in the Arkansas Army National Guard. Her performance in the unit was recognized by Lieutenant General Luck, Commanding General of the 18th Airborne Corps.

Information obtained from *Patchwork of Our Lives Women's Recognition Day 1992*

Lieutenant Colonel
Marsha R. Claybrook

First Female Lieutenant Colonel
Arkansas Air National Guard

Lieutenant Colonel (Lt. Col.) Marsha R. Claybrook was the Chief for Nursing Services for the 189th USAF Clinic. She was the first female to achieve the rank of Lieutenant Colonel with the Arkansas Air National Guard.

Lt. Col. Claybrook was deployed to Northern England at Nocton Hall as part of the 310th Contingency Hospital during Operation Desert Storm.

In civilian life, Lt. Col. Claybrook was a Nurse Practitioner at the North Little Rock VA Hospital. She worked with long-term psychiatric patients and those with substance abuse problems.

Information obtained from *Patchwork of Our Lives Women's Recognition Day 1992*

Lieutenant Colonel Brenda Cluck

**First Female Commander Headquarters
and Headquarters Battery, 142nd
Field Artillery Brigade**

**First Female Aide-de-Camp to the
Arkansas National Guard
Adjutant General**

Lieutenant Colonel (LTC) Brenda C. Cluck was born in Russellville, Arkansas. She graduated from Russellville High School in 1985. In 1990, she received a Bachelor of Arts Degree in Rehabilitation Science from the Arkansas Tech University in Russellville. She received a Master's Degree in Human Resources from Webster University in 2000.

LTC Cluck began her remarkable military career on June 19, 1985, when she enlisted in the 217th Maintenance Battalion, as a (72E), Radio Teletype (RATT) operator, Arkansas Army National Guard in Russellville. She completed her basic training at Fort. Dix and advanced individual training at Fort Gordon (currently Fort Eisenhower) immediately after graduating high school and prior to enrollment in college. During her assignment at 217th, she spent her first Annual Training in Colorado Springs, Colorado and soon realized the Army National Guard was full of adventure.

This motivated her to enter Class 31 of the Officer Candidate School (OCS) at the Arkansas Military Academy in 1987. After twelve months of instruction, during LTC Cluck's final Army Physical Fitness Test she failed to complete the minimum requirement for sit-ups by one repetition. This was not due to lack of capability, but as a result of competing and achieving her Taekwondo black belt the previous day. Since this was a mandatory requirement for graduation, demonstrating her incredible dedication and perseverance, LTC Cluck promptly marched off the practice field and stepped into the Class 32 formation which was starting that same day. A year later in 1988, LTC Cluck completed the OCS Program and received her commission as 2nd Lieutenant, Signal Corps. Her 'Never Quit' mentality followed her throughout her career.

After commissioning, her first assignment was the Detachment Commander of the 937th Signal Battalion, in Fayetteville. In 1995, LTC Cluck was selected into the Title 32 Active Guard and Reserve (AGR) program as personnel officer for the 937th Signal Battalion. In early 1996, the 937th Signal Battalion was deactivated, and she was transferred to the 142nd Field Brigade where she was assigned as the first female Headquarters and Headquarters Battery (HHB) Commander. In March 1997, she was reassigned to 87th Troop Command serving as the personnel officer for the brigade-size element. The 212th Signal Battalion was anxious to get her back to her signal roots and requested her support during their National Training Center rotation in 2000. They succeeded in making her a permanent staff officer 212th Training officer in late 2000. In doing so, this made her part of an amazing female leadership team including then LTC (COL Ret) Carol Johnson as Battalion Commander, and MAJ (COL Ret) Anita Deason as the Battalion Executive Officer. During her first year with 212th she was selected for additional assignment as the first female Aide-de-Camp for Major General Don C. Morrow, the Adjutant General of the Arkansas National Guard.

With her promotion to Major, in 2002 her field grade assignments proved to be even more challenging. She was assigned to the 25th Rear Area Operations Center (RAOC). The unit's unique mission required tremendous coordination with other states to achieve training objectives. In 2002, she was reassigned to the 87th Troop Command as the personnel officer, but it was short lived as the entire state prepared for mobilization of the 39th Infantry Brigade Combat Team. LTC Cluck was recruited to lead the unit's Joint Visitors Bureau deploying with the unit on October 12, 2003, for Operation

Iraqi Freedom. The mobilization lasted until April 2005. This included pre-deployment training at the Joint Readiness Training Center at Fort. Polk, Louisiana. She was called to duty quickly and supported a visit from President George W. Bush. Her first direct engagement with enemy forces came during the convoy movement of the Brigade Headquarters Company from Kuwait to Baghdad, when her serial was engaged in an ambush. She received the Combat Action Badge for this engagement. Her responsibilities in Iraq included planning and executing a visit from the Chairman of the Joint Chiefs of Staff, General Peter Pace. Due to increased combat operations, visitors decreased, and she was assigned additional duties such as pay officer and support to the brigade civ-mil operations. This assignment gave her an incredibly unique opportunity to interact regularly with the budding Iraqi government and many civilians. She befriended Iraqi translators and got an intimate perspective of Iraqi culture, this also put her in some equally dangerous situations. She was always 'cool as cucumber' and served her country valiantly.

Upon return from mobilization, she was assigned to lead the Officer Branch in the Deputy Staff Personnel (DSPER) Office, Joint Forces Headquarters. In this position she literally assisted hundreds of officers in their career progression. She served as the State's Joint Services Support, Branch Chief from 2010 until her retirement in 2013. In this position she assisted thousands of Soldiers and their families.

Her military education includes U.S. Army Basic Course, Communications Electronics Individual Advanced Training, NBC Defense Course, Master Fitness Course, Signal Officer Basic Course, Signal Officer Advanced Course, Command and General Staff Officer Course, the US Army Human Resources Management Course, and the Company/Battery Command Course.

LTC Cluck's career was marked with distinction through the receipt of the following awards, decorations and honors to include the Legion of Merit Medal, Meritorious Service Medal, Army

Commendation Medal, Army Achievement Medal, Army Reserve Components Achievement Medal, National Defense Medal, Global War on Terrorism Expeditionary Medal, Global War on Terrorism Service Medal, Armed Forces Reserve Medal, Army Service Ribbon, Arkansas Federal Service Ribbon, Arkansas Service Ribbon, Army Reserve Component Training Ribbon, Arkansas Emergency Service Ribbon, the Arkansas Distinguished Service Ribbon and the combat action badge.

In April 2013, LTC Cluck retired after over 27 years of outstanding military service.

LTC Cluck and her husband COL (Ret) Damon Cluck are both retired and reside in North Little Rock with their three lovely children Annabel, Aiden, and Hayden.

Command Sergeant Major
Deborah J. Collins

**First Female Instructor
NCO Academy Staff
(Regional Training Institute)**

**First Female President of the Enlisted
Association of the
Arkansas National Guard**

**First Female State
Command Sergeant Major**

Command Sergeant Major (CSM) Collins was born September 15, 1956, in Booneville, Arkansas. She is a 1974 graduate of Russellville High School, Russellville, Arkansas.

CSM Collins began her military career when she enlisted as a private in Headquarters, Headquarters Detachment, 217th Maintenance Battalion, Arkansas Army National Guard on July 30, 1975. She attended Basic Training at Fort Jackson, South Carolina where she served as a Squad Leader in her Platoon and then attended Radio Teletype Operator (05F10) Advanced Individual Training at Fort Gordon, Georgia. Upon her return from training, she was the Radio Teletype Team Chief until November 1978. She was then selected and reassigned to the Noncommissioned Officer (NCO) Academy Staff as an Instructor. She was the first female instructor on the newly formed NCO Academy Staff which is the present-day Regional Training Institute. CSM Collins served in multiple positions on the NCO Academy Staff from November 1978 until May 1990. She was also active in the Enlisted Association of the Arkansas National Guard and became the first female president of the association in 1983. CSM Collins was promoted to Master Sergeant with her duty assignment being Deputy Commandant on

November 26, 1988. She was the first female MSG in the Arkansas Army National Guard. She served in this capacity until May 11, 1990, when she was appointed to 1SG/Deputy Commandant. 1SG Collins then transferred on June 11, 1990, and became the 1SG of the 119th Personnel Services Company. She served in this capacity until January 1991, when she did a permanent change of station (PCS) to attend the United States Army Sergeants Major Academy (USASMA) Resident Course – Class 37. She was the first female from Arkansas Guard to attend USASMA. CSM Collins graduated in July 1991 in the top 10% of her class and returned to the state.

In January 1992, CSM Collins was selected for the CSM position of the 212th Signal Battalion and was promoted to Command Sergeant Major on April 1, 1992. She was the first female Command Sergeant Major in the state. She served as the Battalion CSM from January 1992 until October 1996. While serving as the Battalion CSM, she was selected to be the NCOIC of the Task Force for the 1993 Presidential Inauguration Parade for President Bill Clinton. The task force consisted of Soldiers from every unit in the state and the 106th Army Band.

On November 1, 1996, she was reassigned to 87th Troop Command as the Brigade Operations SGM (the first female Brigade Ops SGM) and laterally appointed to SGM. During this time, she was instrumental in developing the certification training required for the deployment of the 296th Ambulance Service Company to Bosnia.

On September 1, 1992, SGM Collins was laterally appointed back to CSM and was assigned to the Camp Robinson Maneuver Training Center as the Post CSM. She served in this capacity until June 4, 1998, when the 87th Troop Command Commander selected her for the 87th Troop Command CSM position. Again, the first female to serve as a CSM at brigade level. 87th Troop Command was the most diverse Brigade in the state, consisting of a signal battalion, engineer battalion, two aviation battalions, a Rear Area Operations Center along with several stand-alone companies. CSM Collins served with

65

four commanders as the CSM, to include COL Carol Johnson making them the first female command team at Brigade level. CSM Collins remained the Brigade CSM until March 2003.

CSM Collins full-time technician career paralleled her military career until her selection as the State CSM. She was hired as a full-time employee on October 3, 1976. She worked in the Comptroller section until her selection as an Auditor for the Internal Review Section at the United States Property & Fiscal Office. She was the first female ever selected for this position. She remained in this position until 1993 when she was reassigned to the Arkansas Military Academy (AMA) as the Training Technician. She worked at AMA until the Personnel Officer selected her as the Training and Development Specialist for the Human Resources Office (HRO). She also held the Employee Relations Specialist and then was selected as the Classification Specialist for HRO. She was the first female to hold this position in the state. She worked as the Classification Specialist at HRO until The Adjutant General selected her as the State CSM.

CSM Collins assumed the duties of State Command Sergeant Major on March 3, 2003. She was the third female State CSM in the nation. During her tenure, she served on the Army National Guard of the United States CSM Advisory Council from 2004-2011 culminating with her election to the Chair position in 2009, the first female to lead this advisory council. CSM Collins was instrumental in overseeing the centralized promotion system development for the Army National Guard while serving on the council. She established four programs that continue to operate today: the Recruit Sustainment Program, the State Performance Orientated Soldier and NCO of the Year competition, and the Military Funeral Honors Program.

CSM Collins retired as a full-time employee for the Arkansas National Guard in November 2011 with over 35 years of service, but her service was not complete. The Adjutant General selected

CSM Collins to serve as the first Senior Enlisted Leader (SEL) of the state. This was due to reorganization and development of a Joint Staff at Headquarters and the restructuring of the entire command staff. CSM Collins served as a traditional guardsman as the SEL until her retirement from the Arkansas Army National Guard on July 30, 2014, with 39 years of service.

CSM Collins was inducted into the Arkansas National Guard Enlisted Hall of Fame on May 1, 2021. She was the first female and the first Army inductee. CMS Collins was inducted into the Arkansas Military Veteran's Hall of Fame on November 4, 2023. She was the first female enlisted person to be inducted into the ARMVHOF.

CSM Collins has received the following awards and decorations: Legion of Merit with Bronze Oak Leaf Cluster; Meritorious Service Medal with Silver and Bronze Oak Leaf Clusters; Army Commendation Medal with 2 Bronze Oak Leaf Clusters; Army Achievement Medal; Good Conduct Medal; Army Reserve Component Achievement Medal with Silver and 4 Bronze Oak Leaf Clusters; National Defense Service Medal with Bronze Star Device; Global War on Terrorism Service Medal; Armed Forces Reserve Medal with Gold Hour Glass; Noncommissioned Officer Professional Development Ribbon with Numeral 4; Army Service Ribbon; Arkansas Distinguished Service Medal, Arkansas Exceptional Service Medal; Arkansas Commendation Medal with 3 Bronze Diamond Devices; the Arkansas Military Funeral Honors Service Ribbon; and the Arkansas Service Ribbon with 1 Silver and 1 Bronze Diamond Devices.

CSM Collins' military education includes: the U.S. Army Sergeants Major Academy Resident Course Class 37; First Sergeant Course-Reserve Components (RC); Senior NCO Battle Staff Course-RC; Advanced Noncommissioned Officers Course-Active Component (AC); United States Army Sergeants Major Academy Instructor Training Course-RC; Basic Noncommissioned Officers Course-RC; and Radio Teletype Operator-05F Course-AC.

CSM Collins is a lifetime member of the Enlisted Association of the National Guard of the United States and the Enlisted Association of the Arkansas National Guard. She is married to George "Mike" Collins of Rogers, Arkansas and they have one son, Brent.

Colonel Anita E. Deason

**First Female Battalion
Administrative Officer**

**First Female Human Resources Officer
Arkansas Army National Guard**

Colonel (COL) Anita E. Deason was born September 23, 1960, in Little Rock, Arkansas. She is a 1978 graduate of Mayflower High School. COL Deason received her Bachelor's Degree in Liberal Arts from the University of Arkansas at Little Rock and her Master's Degree in Public Administration from Webster University.

COL Deason began her service to the Arkansas National Guard as a state employee in August 1978. She began her military career with the Arkansas Army National Guard as a Private First Class, E-3, on December 13, 1979. During her enlisted service, she worked full-time for the Director of Personnel and Administration and the Support Personnel Management Office. She was the first female Battalion Administrative Officer in the Arkansas Army National Guard. Her units of assignment were the 25th Rear Area Operations Center, Command and Control Headquarters and the State Area Command. COL Deason's primary military occupational skill was 75Z, Personnel Sergeant, and her highest enlisted grade held was Sergeant First Class, E-7.

COL Deason graduated from the Arkansas Military Academy, Officer Candidate School (OCS) Class 28 in 1985. After graduating OCS, she continued with her full-time enlisted service, and on April 3, 1989, COL Deason accepted her commission as a Second Lieutenant and branched as a Signal Corps Officer. Her first unit of assignment after commissioning was Company D, 212th Signal Battalion.

COL Deason served in a variety of full-time and traditional command and staff assignments to include: Platoon Leader, Detachment Commander, Company Executive Officer, Company Commander, Battalion Supply Officer (S-4), Battalion Training Officer, Battalion Assistant Operations Officer (A/S-3), Battalion Administrative Officer, and Battalion Executive Officer with the 212th Signal Battalion; as a Junior TAC Officer with the Ohio Military Academy, Ohio National Guard; Personnel Officer for the 87th Troop Command; Training Officer with the Recruiting and Retention Command; Command Group Special Projects Officer, Secretary to the General Staff; and Battalion Commander of the 871st Troop Command. During her final assignment as the Human Resources Officer for the Arkansas National Guard, she was promoted to Colonel, 06, effective December 22, 2010. In this role, COL Deason became the first female Human Resources Officer for the Arkansas National Guard. Also, during her last assignment, COL Deason served as the Chair of the Regional and National Human Resources Advisory Councils.

COL Deason's military education includes the Reserve Component Basic and Advanced Noncommissioned Officer Schools, Active Component Advanced Noncommissioned Officer School, Signal Officer Basic and Advanced Courses, Combined Arms and Services Staff School, and Command and General Staff College.

COL Deason's awards, decorations and badges include the Legion of Merit; Meritorious Service Medal (2nd Award); Army Commendation Medal (2nd award); Army Achievement Medal (2nd Award); Army Good Conduct Medal (3rd Award); Army Reserve Components Achievement Medal (3rd Award); National Defense Service Medal (2nd Award); Global War on Terrorism Service Medal; NCO Professional Development Ribbon (3rd Award); Army Service Ribbon; Armed Forces Reserve Medal with 30 year device; Arkansas Commendation Medal (2nd Award); Arkansas Service Ribbon (6th Award), Arkansas Recruiting and Retention Ribbon, the

Arkansas National Guard General Staff Badge, and the Signal Corps Bronze Order of Mercury.

COL Deason retired with over 33 years of military service on March 31, 2013. In February 2015, COL Deason was selected for the position of Military and Veterans Affairs Liaison for U.S. Senator John Boozman. On behalf of the Senator, COL Deason worked tirelessly to serve Arkansas veterans, military personnel, and their families. To improve support to our veterans, she increased working relationships with five VA Medical Centers that included Arkansas, Tennessee, Louisiana, and Missouri; 16 VA Community Based Outpatient clinics; and two Vet Centers, the regional Veterans Benefits Administration and the VA and state veteran cemeteries. She communicated with other congressional offices, the Arkansas Department of Veterans Affairs and multiple other offices, agencies, and organizations for a more collaborative effort in suicide prevention, mental health, homelessness, and veteran support overall. She also worked diligently with numerous veteran service organizations and coalitions to stay informed and to provide better outreach across the state. COL Deason regularly visited with leadership from all military installations in Arkansas, as well as Red River Army Depot in Texas to stay current on their readiness levels and abreast of their challenges and concerns. She enhanced connections with the Defense POW/MIA Accounting Agency to provide better support to the families of our heroes and to provide assistance when remains of our heroes were returned home. COL Deason heightened the awareness and support to veteran farmers, businesses, and entrepreneurs. And last, she established a noteworthy relationship with the Library of Congress Veterans History Project resulting in nearly 70 veteran interviews and multiple workshops that COL Deason conducted to train over 1,200 Arkansas to capture and preserve the military experiences of our veterans.

In 2018, COL Deason was inducted into the Arkansas Military Veteran's Hall of Fame.

COL Deason retired from Senator Boozman's office in October 2021, and resides in Conway, Arkansas. She has one son, Zachary Long. He and his wife live in Kyoto, Japan.

Brigadier General
Bobbi J. Doorenbos

First Female Wing Commander and Air Commander of the 188th Wing, Arkansas Air National Guard

Brigadier General (Brig. Gen.) Bobbi J. Doorenbos is an accomplished military leader and trailblazer. Raised in Omaha, Nebraska, she spent her formative years in the heartland of America. After completing seventh grade, she relocated to the small town of Breda, Iowa, which boasted a population of just 500 people. To attend high school, Brig. Gen. Doorenbos had to commute to the nearby Kuemper Catholic High School in Carroll, Iowa.

Brig. Gen. Doorenbos' determinaton and drive continued to shine as she pursued higher education. She earned her Bachelor of Business Studies Degree in Finance from Iowa State University in Ames, Iowa. It was during her time at Iowa State that she honed her skills as a future leader.

In 1992, Brig. Gen. Doorenbos achieved a groundbreaking milestone by becoming the first female F-16 pilot to be hired in the Iowa Air National Guard. Her application for the position was contingent upon the combat exclusion law for females being overturned. In 1993, Brig. Gen. Doorenbos' persistence paid off when the law was indeed changed. Subsequently, she entered the rigorous training pipeline in 1995, embarking on her journey as an F-16 pilot. She was selected for pilot training by the Iowa Air National Guard's 185th Fighter Wing in Sioux City and received her commission through the Academy of Military Science in 1995.

As an F-16 pilot in Iowa, she flew missions in Operation Southern Watch and participated in drug interdiction efforts near South

America. In 2002, she transitioned to the National Guard Bureau at Andrews AFB, Maryland, where she worked on the Crisis Action Team following the attacks of Sept. 11, 2001. She also continued flying the F-16 with the Washington, D.C., Air National Guard (ANG), participating in Operations Noble Eagle and Iraqi Freedom.

As a testament to her bravery and dedication to her country, Brig. Gen. Doorenbos is considered a hometown hero. The Siouxland Freedom Park, a tribute to American veterans, proudly displays a Freedom Rock featuring her portrait. Renowned artist Ray "Bubba" Sorensen II masterfully painted General Doorenbos' likeness on this iconic rock.

Brig. Gen. Doorenbos most recently served as Special Assistant to the Director, in the role of Military Deputy for Air Force Training and Readiness. In this role she exercised Deputy-level responsibilities over policy, guidance, and oversight of Air Force operational training infrastructure, officer and enlisted operations career field management, operational readiness and reporting, and aircrew management. Prior to that, beginning in January 2015, Brig. Gen. Doorenbos served as both the Wing Commander and Air Commander for the nearly 1,000 members of the 188th Wing in Fort Smith, Arkansas. In this dual role as Wing Commander and Air Commander, Brigadier General Doorenbos was the first female to oversee all of the 188th Wing's operations and support functions, and managed the full-time force of federal technicians, Active Guard and Reserve members and state employees.

Before taking command of the 188th Wing, Brig. Gen. Doorenbos served as the commander of the 214th Reconnaissance Group, at Davis-Monthan Air Force Base, Arizona. There, she was responsible for providing combat-qualified MQ-1 Predator aircrews in support of contingency operations overseas, and domestic Incident Awareness and Assessment capabilities in the United States.

She previously served as Chief, Program Requirements and Integration Division, National Guard Bureau Plans and Requirements (NGB/A5P) at Andrews Air Force Base, Maryland. She was responsible for the modernization of the Air National Guard's C4ISR, cyber, space, special mission C-130, simulator and Battlefield Airman assets, filling critical combat and domestic capability gaps for warfighters and first responders.

She has held various positions at NGB, including Executive Officer for the Deputy Director, ANG; Chief of the Deployments Execution Branch (ANG/A3XO); White House Fellow; Executive Officer/Speechwriter for the ANG Director; Chief of the Airborne ISR Division (NGB/A2C); and Special Advisor to Vice President Joe Biden for Defense Policy and Intelligence Programs. Brig. Gen. Doorenbos was a senior pilot with more than 1,200 hours in the F-16C and is now a First Officer on the Airbus 320 for American Airlines.

Brigadier General Bobbi J. Doorenbos' extraordinary achievements and tenacity serve as an inspiration to all, breaking barriers and forging a path for future generations.

CSM Gretchen Doty-Evans

First Female First Sergeant of the 239th Military Intelligence Company, 39th Infantry Brigade

First Female First Sergeant of 216th MP Company, 87th Troop Command

Texas native Command Sergeant Major (CSM) Gretchen Evans began her military journey when she entered the United States Army as a private in 1979. CSM Evans first assignment was an Intelligence Analyst for Commander in Chief in Europe. She later returned to the Defense Language Institute in California studying German and Italian and became a Counterintelligence Agent. Following her graduation from language school, CSM Evans attended Basic Airborne training at Fort Benning, Georgia. She served on active duty for ten years. She is a graduate of the Sergeant Majors Academy at Fort Bliss, Texas.

After 10 years on active duty, CSM Evans transitioned to the reserves in 1989. She served in multiple staff positions. She joined the Arkansas National Guard in 1997 where her first assignment was with the 25th Rear Operations Command, as an operational sergeant. She then was promoted to First Sergeant (1SG) in January 1999 and became the first female 1SG of the 239th Military Intelligence Company as part of the 39th Infantry Brigade. She later transferred to 87th Troop Command and on November 20, 2000, was the first female 1SG of the 216th Military Police Company.

CSM Evans was promoted to Command Sergeant Major on April 1, 2002, and was assigned to the 212th Signal Battalion, being the second female CSM in the Arkansas National Guard. She then inter-state transferred to the Texas National Guard.

CSM Evans held leadership roles in multiple combat engagements and had several other deployments during her 27 years in the Army. As the CSM during her final assignment with Commander, Combined Forces Command-Afghanistan from December 2004 to March 2006, she was responsible for the security and personnel on bases and forwarding operation bases in Afghanistan and oversaw more than 30,000 ground troops.

She earned numerous medals and awards, including the Bronze Star, the Presidential Unit Citation Medal, and Global War on Terrorism ribbons, six Meritorious Service Medals and numerous other awards. In 2006, CSM Evans' world changed in a millisecond when she was severely wounded by incoming fire while serving in Afghanistan. The rocket blast caused her debilitating injuries, including a traumatic brain injury, internal injuries, and the loss of all hearing. After her combat injury, recent PTSD diagnosis and subsequent retirement from service, her transition from military life to civilian life was difficult. With grit, gumption, resilience, and determination CSM Evans navigated through a changed life and found her new passion and purpose which is advocating for veterans of all services.

In 2017, CSM Evans published her first book, *Leading from the Front*, Lessons by a Command Sergeant Major, and in 2018, she co-led a group of youth with mixed abilities on an expedition to Nepal. In 2019, CSM Evans assembled a team of disabled/wounded combat veterans to compete in the World's Toughest Race in Fiji, hosted by Bear Grylls and produced by Mark Burnett (Survivor). Her team, UNBROKEN was the first disabled team to ever compete in the World's Toughest Race. Team UNBROKEN inspired millions with their resolve to not let their injuries define who or what they could achieve in life. Out of 66 teams that competed in the World's Toughest Race, Team UNBROKEN is one of ten teams featured presently on Amazon Prime, World's Toughest Race. CSM

Evans is a nationally known motivational speaker, speaking to both large corporations, businesses, and Veteran centric organizations. She was inducted into the U.S. Veteran Hall of Fame in 2021 and was inducted into the U.S. Army Women's Hall of Fame in March 2020 for her outstanding meritorious service with the United States Army and her community. CSM Evans received the Pat Tillman Award for Service at the ESPY Awards on July 20, 2022.

Gretchen's story is featured in the new 2020 bestselling book, *What's Within You is Stronger Than What is in Your Way*. Gretchen has been featured on the Megyn Kelly Show, the Today Show and CBS Courage in Sports. She also has been highlighted in multiple written media publications. She is an avid hiker, marathon runner, cyclist, and adventure racer. CSM Evans currently resides in Northlake, Texas with her husband Robert, a retired Navy Chaplain, and their two service dogs Aura and Rusty.

Chief Master Sergeant
Glenda Edwards

First Female Chief Master Sergeant
188th Fighter Wing,
Arkansas Air National Guard

Chief Master Sergeant (CMSgt) Glenda Edwards was born in Waldron, Arkansas and graduated from Northside High school in June 1982. Prior to joining the Air National Guard (ANG), she worked various jobs such as accounts receivable/payable, restaurant management, and commercial real estate sales. CMSgt Edwards played softball with members of the 188th on a local league where they prepared to participate in the Air National Guard Tournament. Teammates of the 188th encouraged her to join the ANG to which she did in 1985. She began her career as airman, serving in the military pay section. She was selected for full-time Active Guard and Reserve (AGR) position in 1986 as a commercial services technician, was later promoted to NCOIC of budget and then upgraded to accounting supervisor in approximately 1992.

In 1995, CMSgt Edwards was selected for assignment in the medical group as health system specialist. In October 2002, Edwards became the first female Chief Master Sergeant in the 188th Fighter Wing. In her position as Health Systems Specialist, CMSgt Edwards was responsible for developing plans in support of the overall operation of the medical group. She directed medical group programs such as recruiting mobilization, credentialing, public relations, inspections, investigations, logistics, programs, and mass casualty exercises. She administered the managed care program and provided guidance to the Wing Commander concerning health issues. She prepared the operating budget serving as a member of the Wing financial working group. CMSgt Edwards also served as treasurer for the Wing's Chiefs council. While CMSgt Edwards was in the 188th, she obtained her

Bachelor of Science Degree in Human Resource Management in 1996 and multiple associate degrees.

CMSgt Edwards retired in 2007 and returned to her previous career in real estate. She quickly obtained her broker's license in 2009 and has been principal broker, of River City Realty since. She has been a multimillion-dollar producer since beginning in 2009. In 2023, she began another career selling Aflac Supplemental insurance while still selling real estate. CMSgt Edwards highly encourages participation in the 188th and says when she joined in 1985, her career goals were undefined, she found a family atmosphere, with structure and a lot of growing potential in the 188th. She is thankful for the men and women she was blessed to serve with.

Lieutenant Colonel
Peggy Frye

First Female Lieutenant Colonel
188th Fighter Wing,
Arkansas Air National Guard

Lieutenant Colonel (Lt. Col.) Peggy Frye was born November 16, 1940, in Yoestown, Arkansas. She graduated from Van Buren High School in 1959, and then from Sparks School of Nursing R.N. Program in 1962. She later completed her Bachelor of Science in Nursing in 1987 from Saint Joseph's College. She received her commission in 1974 United States Air Force – Nurse Corp and served 23 years with the 188th Medical Squadron. She retired as Nursing Coordinator at LeFlore County Health Dept. Lt. Col. Frye was the first female of the 188th Wing to be promoted to the rank of Lieutenant Colonel. Lt. Col. Frye was promoted on December 14, 1989, and was a member of the 188th Medical Training Squadron.

Colonel Mary Tenise Gardner

First Female Group Commander 188th Wing, Arkansas Air National Guard

Colonel (Col.) Mary Tenise Gardner was born in Fort Smith, Arkansas. She enlisted in the Arkansas Air National Guard in 1987 and was assigned to the Public Affairs Office as an Administrative Assistant. In 1989, she moved to the Social Actions Office as the Drug and Alcohol Noncommissioned Officer (NCO). In August of 1991, she received her commission from the Academy of Military Science in Knoxville, Tennessee. She became the Human Relations Officer and in 1998, she became the OIC of Social Actions. In 2000, Col. Gardner was selected as the Support Group Executive Officer. On December 1, 2001, she resigned her position in the Public School System to become the Telecommunications Manager and Commander of the Communications Flight. In April of 2012, she was selected as the Mission Support Group Commander, this made her the first female group commander at the 188th Wing.

Col. Gardner retired in July 2021. She returned to Liberty Public School and teaches 8th grade science, language arts and reading.

Colonel Karen D. Gattis

First Female Commander, 172nd Medical Company (Air Ambulance)

First Female Commander, 1-114th Aviation Battalion

First Female Commander, 77th Aviation Brigade

Colonel (COL) Karen D. Gattis was born in Trona, California in 1962. She graduated from Charleston High School in 1981 and received a Bachelor of Science Degree in Math Secondary Education from the University of Arkansas in 1986. She received a Master's Degree in Operations Management from University of Arkansas in 1994.

COL Gattis began her incredible military career as a senior in high school, when she enlisted in the 296th Medical Company, Arkansas Army National Guard, Charleston, Arkansas. She left for basic training a week after her High School graduation. She did a split option and completed Advanced Individual Training (AIT) in the summer of 1982 allowing her to begin college after basic training. She initially served as the NBC NCO for 296th, completing Basic Noncommissioned Officer Course (BNCOC) and achieving the rank of staff sergeant within four years. COL Gattis entered the Arkansas Military Academy Officer Candidate School (OCS), Class 28 in the summer of 1984 and served as the OCS class president. She was commissioned in the Medical Service Corps upon her graduation in 1985. She returned to the 296th and served as a Platoon leader until 1989 when she began the initial entry rotary wing course at Fort. Rucker, Alabama. She completed flight school in August of 1990 graduating with her Army Aviation Wings and UH-1 (Huey) qualification.

COL Gattis went on to pioneer numerous positions in the state aviation arena. She briefly served as a Platoon Leader of the 936th Air Traffic Control (ATC), Camp Robinson, Arkansas, before taking Command, as the first female Commander of Co D 114th (Air Traffic) Company in September 1991. She served in staff positions at 2-114th Aviation Battalion before taking Company Commander HHC 2-114th Aviation in January 1997. That position was quickly followed by an assignment as the first female Company Commander 172nd Medical Company (Air Ambulance) in March 1997. This was a 04 (Major) command. During this two-year command she succeeded in numerous challenges to include integration of USAR Medevac personnel into the ARNG following Army Aviation Transformation eliminating aviation in the USAR. She then transitioned the unit from 15-ship UH-1 (Huey) to 10 ship UH-60 (Blackhawks). The unit was the first in the state assigned Blackhawk helicopters. She had to ensure adequate qualifications of the pilots and within 12 months the unit was supporting the 39th IBCT at Joint Readiness Training Center (JRTC). After additional staff positions with 2-114th Aviation, 35th Aviation Brigade and State Headquarters, COL Gattis became the first female Battalion Commander of 1-114th (GSAB) in August 2003. After a very successful Battalion Command, she was assigned as operations officer for the 35th Aviation Brigade and in March of 2006 she mobilized with a detachment of the 114th, as part of Operation Iraqi Freedom 06-08. She served as flight operations officer at the Udari Army Airfield, in Camp Buehring, Kuwait responsible for the onward integration of all aviation units going into Iraq and their return upon completion of deployment. During the deployment, in June 2006 she became the first female Arkansas Army National Guard pilot to log combat air mission hours. In August of 2007, COL Gattis was assigned as the first female commander of the 77th Theater Aviation Brigade (TAB). COL Gattis was highly regarded as a caring leader and her focus on leadership development proved to be one of her greatest attributes given the success of her subordinates when deployed abroad.

As a testament to her leadership capabilities, in April 2010, she was assigned as the first female Commander of the Marksmanship Training

Center (MTC), a second 06 command. This is a National Guard Bureau center and schoolhouse that is manned by the Arkansas Army National Guard. She also served on state headquarters staff positions to include joint staff, J5, and then the first female Director of Joint Staff (Traditional Soldier) on October 1, 2014, prior to her retirement.

COL Gattis had an equally impressive civilian aviation career. These highlights included running the United Parcel Service (UPS) air logistics operations for Arkansas. She also held numerous fixed wing certifications to include certified flight instructor and airline transport ratings to fly Boeing 767/767, DC-8, and CRJ jet aircraft. She was a commercial airline pilot (Captain) with Pinnacle Airlines dba Northwest Airlink. In 2004 she began a career with the Federal Aviation Administration (FAA) that lasted over 20 years culminating as Division Manager, General Aviation Safety Assurance (GASA). She worked on several national policy initiatives. She was also recognized for her many achievements to include the 2010 Southwest Region Aviation Safety Inspector of the Year, the 2021 Alaskan Regional Administrator Award for Managerial Excellence and Team Safety Champion, and the 2023 Department of Transportation (DOT) Secretary's Team Award for her role in leading the Alaska Safety Initiative Team.

Her military education includes U.S. Army Basic Training, Advanced Individual Training NBC (54E), Basic NCO Course (BNCOC), Medical Service Corps Officer Basic Course, Officer Rotary Wing Aviation Course, Medical Services Corps Officer Advanced Course, Combined Arms Services Staff School, UH-60 Aircraft Qualification Course, Aviation Safety Officer Course, Command and General Staff Officer Course, Pre-Command Course (Battalion and Brigade), and the resident U.S. Army War College, Carlisle Barracks, Pennsylvania.

COL Gattis's career was marked with distinction through the receipt of the following awards, decorations and honors to include the Legion of Merit Medal, Meritorious Service Medal, Army Commendation Medal, Army Achievement Medal, Army Reserve Components Achievement

Medal, National Defense Medal, Global War on Terrorism Expeditionary Medal, Global War on Terrorism Service Medal, Armed Forces Reserve Medal with 'M' device, Army Service Ribbon, Army Reserve Component Overseas Medal, Army Aviator Badge, Senior Army Aviator Badge, Arkansas Service Ribbon, Arkansas Emergency Service Ribbon, Arkansas Distinguished Service Ribbon. She was awarded the bronze Order of Saint Michael medal and was inducted in the Arkansas OCS Hall of Fame in 2016.

COL Gattis retired on July 31, 2015, with over 34 years of military service. She maintained her civilian career with the Federal Aviation Administration until her retirement July 31, 2023.

Lieutenant Colonel
Sharetta Glover

First Female Deputy Commander
61st Civil Support Team
Arkansas National Guard

Lieutenant Colonel (LTC) Sharetta Glover was born in Camden, Arkansas. She graduated from Camden Fairview High School in 2000. LTC Glover graduated with a Bachelor of Science Degree in Biology and a Minor concentration in Chemistry and Military Science from Henderson State University in 2004. She completed her Master's Degree in Public Health from the American Military University in 2017.

LTC Glover began her military career by enlisting in the Arkansas Army National Guard in July 2002 in Company A, 212th Signal Battalion. In August of 2002, she became a Reserve Officers' Training Corps (ROTC) Simultaneous Membership Program (SMP) Cadet at the Henderson State University and Ouachita Baptist University ROTC program. LTC Glover received her commission to Second Lieutenant as an Army Medical Department (AMEDD) Officer upon graduation.

LTC Glover completed the AMEDD Basic Officer Leadership Course in 2005 and the AMEDD Captain's Career Course in 2008. She attended the Human Resources Management Qualification Course in October 2015, and the Intermediate Level Education Course in December 2015. She completed the Advanced Operations Course in September 2018, the Support Operations Course in November 2019, and the Medical Strategic Leader's Course in 2022.

LTC Glover has served in a variety of assignments throughout her career. She served as Operation Officer at the Arkansas Army National Guard Medical Readiness Detachment and later became the unit commander for Arkansas Medical Readiness Detachment before joining the Active Guard/Reserve (AGR) program as the Medical Operations Officer for the 61st Civil Support Team (CST). In 2010, she became the Science Officer for the 61st CST and in 2014 she became the 87th Troop Command Brigade S1. In 2016, she was assigned as the commander of the 213th Medical Company (Area Support) while still filling the role as the Brigade S1 in a full-time capacity. In 2018, she returned to the 61st CST as the Deputy Commander. She was the first female to serve as the Deputy Commander of the 61st Civil Support Team. LTC Glover served as the Personnel Services Branch Chief for the Deputy Chief of Staff-Personnel from June 2020 until June 2021. Her current full-time assignment is the Deputy State Surgeon at the Arkansas Medical Readiness Detachment. As the Deputy State Surgeon, she works with the State Surgeon to manage the medical readiness for all Soldiers in the Arkansas Army National Guard. On July 30, 2023, LTC Glover assumed Command of the 39th Brigade Support Battalion.

LTC Glover is a Past President and former legislative chair of the National Guard Association of Arkansas (NGAA). She is a lifetime member of the NGAA and National Guard Association of the United States. Additionally, LTC Glover is a lifetime auxiliary member of the Enlisted Association of Arkansas National Guard and a member of Association of United States Army. She currently serves as the Treasurer of the Arkansas National Guard Museum Foundation. She is also a member of the Governor's Challenge Team to prevent suicide among service members, veterans, and their families.

LTC Glover's awards and decorations include the Meritorious Service Medal (4th Award), Army Commendation Medal (2nd Award), Army Achievement Medal (5th Award), Army Reserve Component Achievement Medal, National Defense Service Medal,

Global War on Terrorism Medal, Armed Forces Reserve Medal, Army Service Ribbon, Arkansas Service Ribbon (4th Award), Arkansas Emergency Service Ribbon, Tennessee National Guard Commendation Medal, and the Texas Adjutant General Individual Award.

Lieutenant Colonel
Bridgette D. Griffin

First Female Bronze Star Recipient
Arkansas Air National Guard

Lieutenant Colonel (Lt. Col.) Bridgette Delaine Scott Griffin graduated as Salutatorian from Blevins High School in May 1989. She received a Bachelor's Degree in Business Administration Management from Henderson State University in 1996, Bachelor of Science in Nursing from Midwestern State University in 2008 and a Master's Degree of Military Operational Art and Science from Air University in 2018. Since retirement Lt. Col. Griffin has earned her certification in Information Technology and is currently enrolled in the DeVry University Medical Billing and Coding program.

Her stellar military career started in December 1992, when she enlisted as an Airman First Class with the 188th Fighter Wing, Arkansas Air National Guard in Fort Smith. She attended basic training at Lackland Air Force Base, Texas and Technical School at Sheppard AFB, Wichita Falls, Texas where she excelled and achieved the red rope, the highest level a Tech School student leader can obtain. After training, Lt. Col. Griffin returned to the 188th Medical Group where she served as a Medical Service Specialist. In March 1998, Lt. Col. Griffin crossed trained and attended the training course for Clinical Laboratory Specialist at Sheppard AFB, Wichita Falls, Texas. In June 2005, Lt. Col. Griffin was pinned Second Lieutenant. She was enrolled in nursing school at Midwestern State University and working as the Assistant Manager of a Marriot Hotel chain. She was activated on orders during Hurricane Katrina and left her civilian life to become the Officer in Charge of Patient Administration during the evacuation of Hurricane Katrina victims to Fort Chaffee, Arkansas.

In May 2006, Lt. Col. Griffin attended the Health Service Administration Course and was assigned as the 188th Medical Group, Medical Readiness Officer. In June 2010, she deployed to Bagram Airfield, Afghanistan where she was assigned to Task Force MED-East and 455th Expeditionary Medical Group, Craig Joint Theatre Hospital as the Air Force Commander and Army Staff Executive Officer and Public Affairs Representative. After four weeks, she was asked by the commander to stay in the position for one year versus the traditional six months for Air Force members. She was the point of contact for all government and foreign agencies congressional delegation, and distinguished visitors. In December 2010, she was hand selected by leadership to assist President Barack Obama present six Purple Heart Medals to Airmen and Soldiers. During this time, Lt. Col. Griffin was awarded the Bronze Star Medal becoming the first female of the Arkansas Air National Guard to earn this medal.

In November 2013, she become the full time 188th Medical Group Administrator where she had oversight of all members medical records as the Wing converted from a fighter unit to a remotely piloted aircraft unit. In June 2016, Lt. Col. Griffin accepted a position at the National Guard Bureau, Temple Army National Guard Readiness Center, Arlington, Virginia. She served as the Executive Officer to the Directorate of Domestic Operations. In June 2018, she returned to Arkansas and was assigned as the Deputy Director of Staff for two years at Camp Joseph T. Robinson, North Little Rock. In January 2020, she became the Executive Officer of the 189th Airlift Wing, Little Rock AFB, Jacksonville, where she served during an unprecedented time of the nation amid a pandemic.

Lt. Col. Griffin's military education includes the Medical Service Specialist, Clinical Laboratory Specialist, Medical Laboratory Technician, Airman Leadership School, Reserve Commissioned Officer Training, Health Service Administration Course, Medical Readiness Officer Course, Squadron Officer School, and Air Command and Staff Course.

Her awards and decorations include the Bronze Star Medal, Defense Meritorious Service Medal, Meritorious Service Medal, Air Force Commendation Medal, Air Force Achievement Medal, National Defense Service Medal, Afghanistan Campaign Medal, Global War on Terrorism Expeditionary Medal, Global War on Terrorism Service Medal, Air Force Overseas Ribbon, Air Force Longevity Service and Armed Forces Reserve Medal. In 2014, Lt. Col. Griffin earned the NAACP Roy Wilkins Renowned Service Award.

Lt. Col. Griffin retired in January 2023 after 30 years of service. She enjoys spending time with her husband of three years Jonathan Griffin in their home in Missouri City, Texas. Lt. Col. Griffin travels back to Arkansas regularly to take care of her parents Bennie and Sally Scott, ensuring their appointments are up to date and taken care of. She volunteers with Harris County Justice of the Peace Judge Wanda Adams Eviction Court as one of their resource advocates. She also finds time to sub teach with Fort Bend Independent School District. She is a Lifetime Member of NGAA and Lifetime Associate of EANGUS. Lt. Col. Griffin is a member of New Faith Church in Houston, Texas.

First Sergeant Patricia (Woodburn) Halbert

First Female First Sergeant
142nd Brigade Signal Company,
142nd Field Artillery Brigade

First Sergeant (1SG) Patricia Halbert was born in Hot Springs, Arkansas. She graduated from Cutter Morning Star High School in 2001. 1SG Halbert began her military career by enlisting in the Arkansas Army National Guard in May 2001 in Company B, 212th Signal Battalion.

In April 2002, 1SG Halbert completed Basic Training at Fort Leonard Wood, Missouri and in June of 2002, completed AIT at Fort Gordon, Georgia for 31L Cable Installer Maintainer. In August 2005, she was called up to support in Hurricane Katrina relief and assisted at her unit for a month to assist before assisting in Louisiana for two months. In April 2007, she went on to attend 88M Motor Transport Operator Reclassification Course with 515th Regiment in Santa Fe, New Mexico. In November 2007, 1SG Halbert attended the Warrior Leadership Course at Camp Ashland, Nebraska; then in August 2009, she attended the Basic Noncommissioned Officers Course at Camp Ripley, Minnesota. 1SG continued her training by attending Phase One of the Advanced Leadership Course at Fort Eustis, Virgina and then completed Phase Two in August 2013. In February 2017, she attended the Equal Opportunity Advisor Reserve Component Course at Patrick Air Force Base, Florida and in May 2018, the Senior Leadership Course at Fort Gordon. Due to last minute COVID restrictions, she attended the two-week Master Leadership Course via remote training through Fort Bliss, Texas.

1SG Halbert has served in a variety of assignments throughout her career. In June 2003, she deployed State side in support of Operation Noble Eagle III, to Fort Sam Houston, Texas. In August 2004, she moved to Company B 212th Signal as Senior Cable Systems Installer-Maintainer in North Little Rock. After the 212th disbanded in the beginning of 2006, she took a position at Company E 39th BSB moving back to her original unit location in Benton, as a Vehicle Driver, later reclassing to 88M in mid-2007. In December 2009 1SG Halbert moved into a Squad Leader position at Detachment 2 Company A 39th BSB in Pine Bluff. In July 2014, she promoted to Platoon Sergeant at Det 2 Company A in White Hall. In September 2016, 1SG Halbert returned to her Signal MOS and transferred to the 39th Brigade S6 shop as the Network Operations Chief. She deployed in May 2017 as the 39th Infantry Brigade's Equal Opportunity Advisor to Camp Bondsteel, Kosovo. She became the Operations NCO at the Institute Support Unit at Camp Robinson in August 2019; eventually, moving to Range Control a year later in 2020. In August 2021 1SG Halbert became the first female First Sergeant in the 142nd Field Artillery Brigade, going to 142nd Brigade Signal Company as their First Sergeant.

1SG Halbert's awards and decorations include the Meritorious Service Medal (2nd Award), Army Commendation Medal (4th Award), Army Achievement Medal (5th Award), Army Reserve Component Achievement Medal (6th Award), National Defense Service Medal, Armed Forces Expeditionary Medal, Armed Forces Service Medal, Humanitarian Service Medal, Armed Forces Reserve Medal (2nd Award with "M" device), NATO Medal, Army NCO Professional Development Ribbon (4th Award), Army Service Ribbon, Army Overseas Service Ribbon, Driver and Mechanic Badge, Global War on Terrorism-Service Medal, Arkansas Federal Service Ribbon, Arkansas Service Ribbon (4th Award), Arkansas Emergency Service Ribbon, and Mississippi Emergency Service Ribbon.

SFC Virgina Harris

First Female in the 39th Brigade

SFC Virginia Harris was born in Danville, Arkansas, but moved to California when she was 5. She grew up and went to school there and graduated from East Nicolaus High School in 1964, and then went to the University of Southern California (1964-1968).

In 1968, she joined the military in California, and worked at the U.S. Army Personnel Center, Oakland, California. Her duties were to process soldiers going to and returning from Vietnam. In 1972, she moved back to Arkansas and in February 1974, she joined the Arkansas Army National Guard under the Civilian Acquired Skills Program (CASP), as a member of the 39th Infantry Brigade Headquarters. She was the first female to become a member of the 39th Brigade.

Women in the Brigade was very new to them, and they didn't know how to treat her, especially during Field Training Exercises (FTX) and Annual Training. That first year was a real learning experience. She attended an FTX at Camp Robinson the month after joining, and since there were "no facilities" for females, she would go to the field during the day; then they would bring her back to the cantonment area and would be able to go home for the night. Someone would come back in the morning to pick her up and take her back to the field for the day. When she went to Annual Training at Fort Chaffee, the same thing happened.

After two years with the Brigade Headquarters, she transferred to 39th Support Battalion at Camp Robinson. There were other females in this unit and after a lot of begging and negotiating the women convinced the Commanding Officer that they could do their jobs better if they were allowed to stay overnight in the field and that they would be perfectly safe. It was a learning curve for everyone. The women had to prove that they were capable of doing their jobs, and for the men to accept that they were just as patriotic as they were in wanting to serve our country.

In 1979, SFC Harris transferred to the 455th Transportation Battalion as the Personnel Noncommissioned Officer (NCO), and in 1981 she transferred to State Area Command where she remained until her retirement in 2006.

Shortly after joining the Arkansas Guard, she went to work in the Recruiting and Retention Office (May 1974), on active duty. Then in 1976, she took a Civil Service position at the United States Property and Finance Office (USP&FO) at Camp Robinson in the Finance Office. She stayed with the Finance Office until she retired from Civil Service in 1998, retiring as the Chief, Pay and Exam Branch.

In 1999, SFC Harris participated in a tour in Washington D.C. to assist in working on writing the Defense Integrated Military Human Resources System (DIMHRS) program. Also in her career, she played an active role in sending one of the first National Guard units, the 148th Evacuation Hospital to Saudi Arabia. Her responsibilities included keeping their pay and personnel in the state and not transferring them to active Army. Another role was to help mobilize the 39th Infantry Brigade for Iraq which was the first full bridge from the National Guard to be mobilized.

In 1976, the Adjutant General's office formed a Governor's Color Guard. It was an all-female color guard. It was created with eight original members of which SFC Harris was one. SFC Harris retired in 2006 after serving her country for 35 years.

MSG Dorothy R. Hayner

First Female on Title 10
Active Guard and Reserve Tour

Master Sergeant (MSG) Hayner was born and raised in East Texas. She graduated from Kaniack High School in 1956. There was a strong military influence in her family. SFC Ray W. Fortune, her father, was a veteran of The Great War (WWI). Her brothers, Lewis Fortune (Navy) and Billy B. Fortune (U.S. Army Air Corps), were veterans of WWII. Lewis survived Guadalcanal; Billy retired as USAF Reserve Colonel. Her husband, MSG George H. Hayner, Jr., retired in 1995 with 32 years of active and reserve service. He received the Combat Infantryman Badge (CIB) for service in Vietnam, 1965-1966.

After she complete her Bachelor of Art Degree from East Texas Baptist College in 1972, she taught high school speech and English in Tatum, Texas. As senior class sponsor, she heard the Texas Army National Guard Recruiter speak to her students and realized that a part-time Guard career would enhance her teacher retirement. However, in the spring of 1974, the Air Force Reserve offered her husband a recruiting assignment at Little Rock AFB, Arkansas.

Her first visit to McCain Mall one hot summer night changed her life. She saw an Army National Guard (ARNG) recruiting booth and decided to check it out. The young Sergeant had scant information about a new program for females. He took her name. Good follow-up from Camp Robinson's Recruiting Office resulted in her enlistment on July 23, 1974. Because of her bachelor's degree, she was enlisted as a Private First Class (E-3). Her return from Basic Training was timely. Soon she found herself on a 30-day tour of duty with the Arkansas ARNG.

By 1978, the National Guard Bureau (NGB) had included her in some of the updating and rewording of manuals and documents, making them more inclusive. [Unit sign-in sheets no longer read, "Officers and Men will sign in below."] When she learned that there were opportunities for Title 10 assignments in Europe, she applied for an In-service Recruiter position and was ordered to Title 10 service on January 14, 1980, the first female from the state to go on a Title 10 tour. She was attached to V Corps Headquarters in Frankfurt, West Germany. Her recruiting duties included temporary duty (TDY) trips to Berlin once a month to recruit soldiers for the Reserve Components of the U.S. Army.

The Berlin TDY trips included secure travel through the East German corridor. For the first few visits, she took the duty train; later her and her husband travelled in their POV. She proudly holds the distinction of being the first Arkansas National Guardsman to be declared:

SERGANT FIRST CLASS
DOROTHY R. HAYNER

Having served honorably, East of the Elbe, 110 miles behind the Iron Curtain and in the Shadow of the Wall of Shame and having shared the challenge of maintaining this Outpost of Freedom with our British and French Allies, is hereby declared an honorary lifetime member of Headquarters and Headquarters Company, that unique organization of the Berlin Brigade (Infantry).

Given under my hand seal, this 17th day of FEBRUARY in the Year of Our Lord 1983 in the American Sector of Berlin.

Her retirement plan was to serve twenty-two years. In the summer of 1994, NGB put out the word to Senior NCOs to consider early retirement in the following few months. The Department of Defense

Reduction of Forces was the reasoning behind this appeal. MSG Hayner obliged retiring with 20 years, 5 months, and 8 days of service. She says it took her approximately 24 hours to adjust to retirement.

Chief Warrant Officer Five Pamela Huff

First Female Chief Warrant Officer Five Arkansas Army National Guard

Chief Warrant Officer Five (CW5) Pamela Huff was born in Little Rock, AR. She graduated from Hall High School in 1975, received a Bachelor's Degree in Organizational Management from John Brown University, and a Master of Arts degree in Human Resources Development.

She enlisted in the Arkansas Army National Guard (AR ARNG) in 1975 as a private (PV1). Throughout her career, she served in a variety of assignments. Her first duty assignment was with the 204th Dental Detachment, where she received the Humanitarian Service Medal for the Fort Chaffee Cuban Relocation Operation. She continued her assignments as a Personnel Clerk in the 39th Infantry Brigade; State Area Command (STARC), Arkansas Military Academy as an Admin Supply Clerk and Training Technician. Her next assignment was with the 119th Personnel Service Company where she made a major decision to become a Warrant Officer. In 1990, she became a Warrant Officer and in 1991 was Mobilized with the 119th Personnel Service Company to replace Alpha Battery, Headquarters as the Personnel Records Chief, and the Officer in Charge (OIC) of the Mobilization Out-processing Center at Fort Sill Oklahoma, mobilizing over 4,000 soldiers both active and reserve component. While there she received the Army Commendation Medal.

CW5 Huff continued her military career and was promoted to Chief Warrant Officer Five in 2010, becoming the first female CW5 in the history of the Arkansas Army National Guard. CW5 Huff's military awards include the Meritorious Service Medal, Army Commendation Medal, Army Achievement Medal, Army Reserve Component Achievement Medal (11), National Defense Service Medal (2), Humanitarian Service Medal, Armed Forces Reserve Medal (4), Army Forces Reserve Medal with "M" Device, Noncommissioned Officer Professional Development Medal (3), and the Army Service Ribbon. CW5 Huff's State awards include the Arkansas Commendation Medal, Arkansas Federal Service Ribbon, and Arkansas Service Ribbon (7). CW5 Huff retired from the Arkansas Army National Guard in 2017.

During CW5 Huff's military career, she also became a full-time Federal Technician working for the AR ARNG in 1983. CW5 Huff moved up the ladder during her Federal Technician tenure from a General Scheduled four (GS-4) to a GS-13 where she retired in 2017 as the ARNG's Supervisor/Director over the Internal Review's Audit Division.

After retiring in 2017, CW5 Huff returned in 2018 to work for the Arkansas Army National Guard as a Civilian Contractor as the Suicide Prevention Program Manager and Alcohol/Drug Coordinator.

Major Kimberly M. Hunter

First Female Director of Operations, 188th Intelligence Support Squadron Arkansas Air National Guard

Major (Maj.) Kimberly Hunter was raised in the State of Arkansas and graduated from Cabot High School in 2000. She decided to enlist in the Arkansas Air National Guard as an Imagery Analyst with the 123rd Intelligence Squadron (123 IS), located at Little Rock Air Force Base on February 2, 2002. She attended Intelligence Apprentice school at Goodfellow AFB in San Angelo, Texas and graduated in August of 2003. Meanwhile, as an enlisted drill status guardsman, Major Hunter attended Harding University and earned her bachelor's degree in 2006. Once she graduated college, she was activated in support of Secretary of Defense contingencies, Operation Iraqi Freedom, and Operation Enduring Freedom with Distributed Ground Station (DGS)-Arkansas from June 2006 through August 2009. During that time, she served as an Intelligence Evaluator for the Imagery Analyst, Imagery Screener, and Imagery Mission Supervisor crew positions and as a certified Instructor Rated Operator. In addition to those roles, she instructed and evaluated members from DGS Indiana and Massachusetts allowing both units to reach Initial Operating Capability.

In 2010, a 7.0 magnitude earthquake devastated Haiti. Major Hunter volunteered to be one of the first seven Arkansans sent to Haiti, in support of Operation Unified Response where we were responsible for analyzing infrastructure such as roadways, sea and aerial ports to help identify their capabilities to accept incoming support.

In 2011, Major Hunter commissioned as an officer in the 123rd IS. She attended Intelligence Officer School and graduated in 2012. Upon returning to the 123rd IS, she was activated as a Mission Operations Commander at DGS-AR. In 2015, she transferred to the 288th

Operations Support Squadron (OSS) at Ebbing Air National Guard Base (ANGB) in Fort Smith. As the Chief of Training, she set up the training shop and oversaw the training of newly gained personnel after the 188th Wing Conversion. In 2020, she moved to the 153rd IS, also located at Ebbing ANGB, as the Cyber Systems Flight Commander. Simultaneously, she oversaw the move from Initial Operation Capabilities (IOC) operations in the temporary facility to Full Operation Capabilities (FOC) operations in the ROC for both the ISRG and OG. In 2022, she became the first female Director of Operations for the 188th Intelligence Support Squadron. Major Hunter was selected to command the 188th Communications Squadron in November 2023, where she continues to serve.

Brigadier General
Tamhra L. Hutchins-Frye

First Female Brigadier General
Arkansas Air National Guard

First Female Commander
188th Mission Support Flight

First Female Full-Time
Director Joint Staff
Joint Force Headquarters, Arkansas

Brigadier General (Brig. Gen.) Tamhra Lynne Hutchins-Frye graduated from Lavaca High School in May 1979. She received a Bachelor of Science in Elementary Education from Arkansas Tech University in 1983, and a Master of Art in Human Resource Management from Webster University in 2012.

Her outstanding military career started in 1984 when she enlisted as an Airman First Class in the Personnel career field, with the 188th Fighter Wing, Arkansas Air National Guard in Fort Smith. She was commissioned in 1989 through the Academy of Military Science, Knoxville, Tennessee. She has served in various command and staff positions throughout her career in traditional, Active Guard Reserve (AGR), Dual-Status Technician, Title 10 Active Duty, and Statutory tour status.

In December 1994, Brig. Gen. Hutchins-Frye assumed command of the 188th Mission Support Flight. She was the first female Commander of the 188th Mission Support Flight

Brig. Gen. Hutchins-Frye had to opportunity to mobilize in 2013 as the Chief of Staff, North Atlantic Treaty Organization Afghanistan

Transformation Task Force Then Non-Security Ministries Ministerial Advisory Group, Headquarters International Security Assistance Force, Kabul, Afghanistan.

In February 2015, Brig. Gen. Hutchins-Frye became the first female to serve as the full-time Director of Joint Staff, Joint Force Headquarters, Arkansas National Guard. She was the state's senior federal full-time National Guard management official. She served as the principal executive assistant and advisor to the Adjutant General and was responsible for managing both joint military and full-time functions throughout the state, over-seeing approximately 2,000 full-time personnel.

In December of 2015, Brig. Gen. Hutchins-Frye became the first female Brigadier General for the Arkansas Air National Guard.

Her last military assignment was serving as the Director for Manpower, Personnel and Services, Air National Guard Readiness Center, Joint Base Andrews, Maryland.

Brig. Gen. Hutchins-Frye served as the senior Air National Guard officer responsible for comprehensive plans and policies covering all life cycles of personnel management, which included advocacy at higher headquarters, end strength management, education and training, resource allocation, and the services program on behalf of the 105,700 Airmen.

Her awards and decorations include the Legion of Merit, Bronze Star Medal, Distinguish Service Medal, Meritorious Service Medal, Air Force Commendation Medal, Air Force Achievement Medal, National Defense Service Medal, Afghanistan Campaign Medal with Bronze Star, Humanitarian Service Medal. General Hutchins-Frye is a member of the National Guard Association for Arkansas and United States, the Women's Foundation of Arkansas, Charter member of Women in Military Service for America Memorial Foundation, Girls of Promise.

Brig. Gen. Hutchins-Frye retired on August 1, 2019.

Colonel Erica L. (Johnson) Ingram

**First Female Installation Commander
Camp J.T. Robinson Maneuver
Training Center
Arkansas Army National Guard**

Colonel (COL) Ingram was born in Wilmar, Arkansas, and is a 1990 graduate of Wilmar High School. She graduated from the University of Arkansas at Pine Bluff in May 1995 where she completed the four-year Army ROTC Scholarship program. She received her degree in Business Management with a minor in Administration. COL Ingram received her commission as a Second Lieutenant in the United States Army on August 15, 1995. While serving on Active Duty she was assigned as the Warrior Brigade Assistant Personnel Officer, 5th Personnel Services Battalion Operations/Training Officer and Headquarters Detachment Commander as well as Amarillo Military Entrance Processing Station (MEPS) Test Control Officer and Operations Officer. After serving four and a half years on active duty, she joined the Arkansas Army National Guard on November 11, 1999.

COL Ingram served as Camp Joseph T. Robinson Maneuver Training Center (RMTC) Installation Commander until October 2021. In that assignment, she was the first female to serve as the Commander of the Camp Robinson Maneuver Training Center. Her previous positions within the Arkansas Army National Guard include serving as the 212th Signal Battalion Training Officer, Battalion Administrative Officer, Battalion Personnel Officer, Battalion Operations Officer, 87th Troop Command Brigade Personnel Officer, Recruiting and Retention Command Officer Strength Manager and Executive Officer, Deputy Chief of Staff Personnel Services Branch Chief, Deputy Personnel (G-1), Arkansas National Guard G-1, Deputy State Surgeon - Administrative

Officer, 87th Troop Command Brigade Administrative Officer, and 871st Troop Command Battalion Commander.

Her awards and decorations include the Legion of Merit with one Oak Leaf Cluster, Meritorious Service Medal with eight Oak Leaf Clusters, Joint Service Commendation Medal, Army Commendation Medal with one Oak Leaf Cluster, Army Achievement Medal, Army Reserve Components Achievement Medal, National Defense Service Medal, Army Service Ribbon, Global War on Terrorism Service Medal, Arkansas Emergency Service Ribbon, and Arkansas Service Ribbon.

She is a life member of the National Guard Association of Arkansas (NGAA) and the National Guard Association of the United States (NGAUS) and former NGAA President. She is a Greater Leadership of Little Rock program alumnus and a 2022 Arkansas King-Kennedy Lifetime Achievement Award recipient.

COL Ingram retired from the Arkansas Army National Guard on February 1, 2022. After retirement, she worked as the Chief of Staff/Assistant Director for the Arkansas Department of Veteran Affairs. She currently serves as the Integrated Primary Prevention Program Manager for the Arkansas National Guard.

Colonel Carol A. Johnson

First Female Detachment Commander, Headquarters and Headquarters Company, 39th Support Battalion

First Female Commander, 212th Signal Battalion

First Female Commander, 87th Troop Command

Colonel (COL) Johnson is a native of Kentucky. She began her military career as the first female commissioned officer in the Kentucky Army National Guard when she received a direct appointment as a Second Lieutenant on March 12, 1976. She subsequently attended the Women's Army Corps (WAC) Officer Orientation and Officer Candidate Course at Fort McClellan, Alabama later in 1976.

She transferred from the Women's Army Corps to the Quartermaster Corps in December 1978. She served with the Kentucky Army National Guard as a Supply Distribution Officer, Headquarters and Headquarters Company (HHC), 103rd Support and Service Battalion from 1976 to 1977. She served as General Support Platoon Leader for the 303rd General Support Company from 1977 to 1980. She also served as an Automated Data Processing Officer for HHC, 103rd Support Battalion from 1980 to 1981.

In March 1981, COL Johnson transferred to the Arkansas Army National Guard. She completed the Company Size Unit Commander's Course and became the first female in the Arkansas Army National Guard to assume command when she was assigned at Detachment Commander and Automated Data Processing Officer for Det 1,

HHC, 39th Support Battalion. She served there from 1981 to 1985. She went on to serve with the 39th Infantry Brigade as a staff office in HHC, 39th Support Battalion and Company A, 39th Support Battalion. In 1986 she was transferred to the State Area Command (STARC) where she served as the first Management Information Systems Officer and Director of Information Management through 1992. In 1993, she was assigned as the Chief Examiner at STARC. In 1998, she became the first female Commander of the 212th Signal Battalion. In 2000 was promoted to Colonel and became the first female Deputy Chief of Staff for Logistics. On October 1, 2001, COL Johnson became the first female Brigade level Commander when she assumed command of the 87th Troop Command. She was also the first non-medical female in the state to achieve the rank of Major (field grade officer) and first non-medical female to serve as a Battalion Commander. She later was selected as the Deputy United States Property and Fiscal Officer.

COL Johnson has attended numerous military schools to include Quartermaster and Signal Advance Course, Command and General Staff College and US Army War College. She also has received numerous awards and recognitions for her tremendous service commemorating her many achievements.

Sergeant Major
Deborah Denise Johnson

**First Female Battalion Operations
Noncommissioned Officer**

**First Female Brigade Full-Time
Operations Seargeant Major**

Sergeant Major (SGM) Deborah Denise Johnson was born in Little Rock, on August 29, 1958, and raised in Southwest Little Rock, the oldest of four children. She attended John L. McClellan High School where she lettered in track her junior and senior year. She graduated from McClellan High School May 28, 1976, but enlisted in the Arkansas Army National Guard March 26, 1976, while still attending High School.

SGM Johnson was one of only a handful of females to attain the rank of Sergeant Major in the Arkansas Army National Guard. She progressed through the ranks and served in numerous assignments as a Traditional Soldier. She began her career as an Administration assistant at the rank of Private Second Class (PV2). She attended Basic Training and Advance Training, at Fort Jackson, South Carolina. She was promoted to Administrative Specialist, attaining the rank of Specialist Five while serving at Headquarters and Headquarters Detachment (HHD) 125th Medical Detachment from March 26, 1976, to August 22, 1983. She was selected to serve in the Active Guard Reserve (AGR) at the National Guard Professional Education Center, Camp Robinson. She served as Personnel Staff Noncommissioned Officer (NCO) as a Sergeant First Class (E7) with the 148th Evacuation Hospital from July 9, 1990 to September 24, 1996. She transferred to the Aviation Brigade and served in various positions to include Readiness NCO at 172nd Medical Company (Air Ambulance), Air Traffic Control Liaison NCO at

HHD 2ⁿᵈ Battalion ATC before her promotion to Master Sergeant (E8). In that capacity she served as Aviation Operations Sergeant with HHC 1-114ᵗʰ Aviation Battalion August 1, 2002, to July 10, 2005. In July 2005 she was promoted to Sergeant Major (SGM/E9) and served as the Brigade Operations SGM for HHC 77ᵗʰ Aviation Brigade. This position selection made her the first female Operations Sergeant Major in the Aviation Brigade. SGM Johnson's Deployments included Desert Shield/Storm, Saudia, Abria, November 20, 1990, to May 6, 1991, and Operation New Dawn, Iraq, February 17, 2011, to January 21, 2012.

Her awards and decorations include: Legion of Merit, Bronze Star (1OLC), Meritorious Service Medal (2OLC), Army Commendation Medal (4OLC), Army Achievement Medal (2OLC), Army Conduct Medal (Silver 2 knots), Army Reserve Component Achievement Medal (3OLC), National Defense Service Medal (w/Bronze Service), Southwest Asia Service Medal, Global War on Terrorism Service (M device), NCO Professional Development Ribbon w/Numeral 4, Army Service Ribbon, Army Reserve Components Overseas Training Ribbon, Kuwait Liberation Medal (Saudia Arabia), Kuwait Liberation Medal (Kuwait), Arkansas Distinguished Service Medal, Arkansas Federal Service, Arkansas Service Ribbon (Silver Diamond), Arkansas Service Emergency Service Ribbon (2 Diamonds), Certificate of Achievement APFT (score300) June 30, 2006, Certificate of Commendation-Outstanding Performance Army Physical Fitness Test June 30, 2006, Physical Fitness Badge.

SGM Johnson expressed that there were many challenges as a female in the military. One challenge was becoming a single mom early in my career and raising my amazing son Joshua. With all these challenges, she was still able to rise above and overcome by putting her faith and hope in the Lord Jesus Christ. She received an abundance of support and guidance received from her parents, MSG Bill and Nancy Terry; her husband, CSM Clayton Johnson; CSM Stanley Hicks; LTC John Woodall; and CSM Deborah Collins. All these and so many others were instrumental in her career. She will always be grateful to each and every one of them for the support offered to her during her career.

Growing up, she always dreamed of wearing combat boots and serving alongside her dad in the Army National Guard. SGM Johnson truly admired and looked up to him in the way he served his country. Her dream came true when she was able to serve with her dad and two younger brothers, in the same unit. They were the first family to serve together in the same unit in the Arkansas Army National Guard.

SGM Johnson was an active member in the Enlisted National Guard Association of Arkansas and Enlisted National Guard Association of the United States. She proudly served in any area that was needed in both associations. She retired on July 31, 2013, with 37 years of service; 5 years as a Traditional Soldier and 32 years as Active Guard Reserve Soldier. Her life now consists of spending quality time with the love of her life, her husband and best friend. They both love hunting, fishing, boating, paddle boarding, kayaking, and finding the best waterfalls. She enjoys gardening, praying, reading, and studying the Bible. She is honored to have time to volunteer at my local church, other organizations and spend quality time with family and friends. She was also honored to serve 37 years for her country and state with outstanding Soldiers and she will never regret the path she chose to serve. If she had the opportunity to choose that path again, she would do it in a heartbeat!

Colonel Jenny Johnson

First Female Executive Officer for the Air National Guard Assistant to the Judge Advocate General of the Air Force

First Female Deputy Staff Judge Advocate, 188th Wing, Arkansas Air National Guard

Colonel (Col.) Jenny Johnson grew up in Dardanelle, Arkansas, and graduated from Dardanelle High School in 1989. She attended Henderson State University where she graduated with a Bachelor of Arts in Political Science in August 1992. From there she attended the University of Arkansas at Little Rock School of Law, finishing her Juris Doctorate in 1995. She married her husband, Dave, in 1991. In 2001, she was accepted into the USAF Jag Corps. She commissioned and entered active duty on February 14, 2001. Her first duty location was Peterson Air Force Base (AFB), Colorado Springs, Colorado, for 3 years where she was Trial Counsel in numerous courts martial, Officer in Charge (OIC) of Adverse Actions, and OIC of Claims and Medical Law.

She later transitioned to the USAF Academy, serving as the Area Defense Counsel until 2005. In 2005, her family changed duty stations to Ramstein AB, Germany, where she served as the Medical Law Consultant for US Air Forces Europe (USAFE), responsible for providing legal advice to 10 Military Treatment Facilities (MTF) and hospitals throughout USAFE until separating from active duty in July 2008 and transferred to the Arkansas Air National Guard and was assigned as the Deputy Staff Judge Advocate to the 188th Wing, making her the first female in this role.

In 2013, she was promoted to Staff Judge Advocate (SJA)where she still resides. In addition to her primary SJA duties, in June 2017, she was selected to be the Executive Officer for the Air National Guard (ANG) Assistant to the Judge Advocate General of the Air Force, where she was also the first female selected for this role. Following this additional duty, she was selected on July 1, 2018, to serve in the National Guard Bureau (NGB) National Additional Duty Program (NADP) as the NADP for Special Victims Counsel. On October 1, 2021, her additional duty transitioned to the NADP for Readiness and Inspections, overseeing all ANG Legal Office UEI inspections.

Col. Johnson and her husband have two grown children and three grandchildren. In her free time, she enjoys quilting, reading, and playing with the grandbabies.

Colonel Shirley L. Jones

First Female Commander of the 125th Medical Battalion Arkansas Army National Guard

Colonel (COL) Jones, a native of Bauxite, Arkansas, was appointed Chief Nurse of the Army National Guard on July 20, 1989. COL Jones has concentrated her efforts toward increasing the critical shortage in specialty areas in nursing. She also emphasized readiness, physical fitness, nursing research, and the enhancement of quality assurance in the practice of nurses.

COL Jones was the first female Commander of the 125th Medical Battalion in the Arkansas Army National Guard, a position she held until July 1989. Commissioned in 1972, she held assignments with the 148th Evacuation Hospital such as Medical Surgical Nurse and ultimately Chief Nurse. In 1986, she was named State Chief Nurse, STARC (-), Arkansas Army National Guard (ARNG).

COL Jones has actively pursued her military education, graduating from Officer Advanced Course, the Command and General Staff College, and the National Defense University. Believing the readiness is the key to military nursing, she has successfully completed courses in Combat Readiness, Combat Stress, Management of Chemical Casualties, and Advanced Nursing Principals. She has received extensive training in Total Quality Management (TQM) and is the Point of Contact for TQM in the National Guard Bureau's Office of the Army Surgeon.

COL Jones graduated from the Arkansas Baptist School of Nursing with a diploma and cum laude from the University of Arkansas at Little Rock with a Bachelor of Art Degree in Psychology and

Sociology. In 1986, she earned a Master of Arts in Health Services Management from Webster University.

During her tenure as Chief Nurse, National Guard Bureau, she has experienced two wars; Operation Just Cause and Operation Desert Shield/Storm. She supported twelve ARNG Hospitals deployed to support Desert Storm. All fourteen hundred ARNG nurses were alerted and 689 were mobilized. COL Jones received the Meritorious Service Medal with Third Oak Leaf Cluster from the active army for her performance during Desert Storm. During her military career, she has earned many military awards and is an active member of many associations.

Master Sergeant
Margarett Amos (Linton)

First Female to Receive the Bronze Star
Arkansas Army National Guard

Master Sergeant (MSG) Margarett "Margo" Linton was born in Simsboro, Louisiana. She attended Crawford High School and graduated from Arcadia High School, Arcadia, Louisiana. She received a Bachelor of Arts Degree in Business Management from Philander Smith College in 2002. MSG Linton is the only one of the 12 children in her family who received a college degree.

MSG Linton's remarkable military career started on September 12, 1973, when she joined the United States Marine Corps. She attended her Marine Corps Basic Training at Parris Island, South Carolina. After basic training, she was transferred to Camp Pendleton, California and worked in the Movement Corps Movement Coordination Center (MCMCC) as a Pay Transportation Clerk. MSG Linton was honorably discharged as a Sergeant (E5) from the U.S. Marine Corps on June 10, 1977. For her outstanding service in the Marine Corps, she received the Good Conduct Medal and a Letter of Appreciation.

Her career with the Arkansas Army National Guard began on September 12, 1978, when she enlisted into Detachment (Det) 1, 172nd Maintenance Company, Russellville, Arkansas. Her assignments included F-E System Repairman, Section Chief and Tank Turret Repairman. On March 1, 1983, she was reassigned to Headquarters and Headquarters Detachment, 217th Maintenance Battalion in Russellville, Arkansas as a Clerk Typist.

MSG Linton was hired as a Legal Clerk in the Arkansas Army National Guard Military Technician Program on March 1, 1983, and assigned to

Headquarters and Headquarters Battery, 142nd Field Artillery Brigade, Fayetteville, Arkansas. On January 1, 1984, MSG Linton was hired into the Active Guard/Reserve (AGR) Program. While assigned to the 142nd Field Artillery Brigade, she worked as an Administrative, Supply and Training Specialist (AST), Legal Clerk and Senior Legal Noncommissioned Officer (NCO).

On September 20, 1990, MSG Linton deployed with the 142nd Field Artillery Brigade to Saudi Arabia in support of Operation Desert Shield/Operation Desert Storm. As a Sergeant First Class (SFC), she was the only female first-line leader during the deployment. MSG Linton has the honor of being the first female in the Arkansas National Guard to receive the Bronze Star during Operation Desert Storm/Shield/Sabre in August of 1991.

On June 1, 1998, MSG Linton was transferred to the Arkansas Army National Guard Maneuver Training Center (ARARNG-MTC), Fort Chaffee. While assigned to ARARNG MTC, she served as an Administration NCO and Range Scheduling NCO. On October 18, 1999, MSG Linton was assigned to Headquarters and Headquarter (-), 39th Infantry Brigade, Little Rock and served as the Chief Legal NCO and Senior Administrative NCO for the 39th Infantry Brigade.

MSG Linton's professional military education includes 64C Vehicle Operator Course, Unit Administrators Course; Basic NCO Academy Course, Legal Specialist Course, Fort Benjamin Harrison, Indiana, Law for Legal Specialist Course, Judge Advocate General School, Charlottesville, Virginia, Primary Leadership Development Course, Camp Beauregard, Louisiana, Basic NCO Course, Fort Benjamin Harrison, Indiana, Automation Security Course, National Guard Professional Education Center, Camp Robinson, Field Artillery Combat Lifesaver Course, Fort Sill, Oklahoma, Advanced NCO Course, Fort Benjamin Harrison, Indiana, Personnel Services NCO Course, NGPEC, Camp Robinson, Equal Opportunity Advisor's Course, Camp Robinson, Equal Opportunity Advisor Reserve Component Course, Defense Equal Opportunity Management

Institute, Patrick Air Force Base, Florida and the Personnel Sergeant's Course, NGPEC, Camp Robinson.

Her awards, decorations and qualifications include the Bronze Star, Meritorious Service Medal (4th Award), Army Commendation Medal, Army Achievement Medal, Army Good Conduct Medal, Army Reserve Components Achievement Medal, Defense Service Medal, Kuwait Liberation Medal, Southwest Asia Service Medal, Armed Forces Reserve Medal, NCO Professional Development Ribbon, Army Service Ribbon, Sharpshooter Marksmanship Qualification Badge with Rifle Bar and the special skill identifier, "Q" for Equal Opportunity Advisor.

MSG Linton retired on September 30, 2002, with over 27 years of exceptional military service. She enjoys spending time with her husband, Harry Amos in their home in Kempner, Texas. She attends Christian House of Prayer Church (CHOP) where she serves as a member of the choir. She is a graduate of the church's Sonship School of the First Born and she volunteers her time by sewing robes for every new class and she sews robes for the 197 covenant churches that are located in Germany, Africa, and the United States. MSG Linton's hobbies are sewing and reading Christian fiction books.

Colonel Tina Lipscomb

First Female Squadron Commander
123rd Intelligence Squadron

Colonel (Col.) Tina Lipscomb was born in Martinez, California and grew up in Southern California. In 1985, Col. Lipscomb's family moved to Ozark, Arkansas, where she graduated from Ozark High School. Col. Lipscomb earned an Organizational Management degree from John Brown University and was the first member of her family to attend college.

On June 7, 1988, Col. Lipscomb enlisted with the Arkansas Army Guard, Paris, Arkansas as a traditional Guardsmen. Col. Lipscomb attended Basic Training at Fort Dix, New Jersey and MOS Training at Fort Lee, Virginia. In June of 1991, Col. Lipscomb transferred to the 188th Fighter Wing, Arkansas Air National Guard (ANG) as a Staff Sergeant (SSgt) in Information Management. In 1998, Col. Lipscomb was selected as an Intelligence Officer for the 188th Fighter Wing, and attended the Academy of Military Science in Knoxville, Tennessee, where she was commissioned as a 2nd Lieutenant in the Arkansas Air National Guard. Col. Lipscomb followed on to Intelligence Officer School, at Goodfellow Air Force Base (AFB), San Angelo, Texas.

In February 2000, Col. Lipscomb transferred to the Air Force Reserves, Tinker AFB, Oklahoma. After seven years, Col. Lipscomb returned to the 188th Fighter Wing, Fort Smith, Arkansas as the Senior Intelligence Officer. In April 2009, Col. Lipscomb transferred to the 189th Airlift Wing, Little Rock AFB as the Budget Officer. On October 1, 2020, Col. Lipscomb transferred to the Joint Force Headquarters, Arkansas Air National Guard as the Air Intelligence Officer. In February 2013, Col. Lipscomb was selected as the first female Commander of the 123rd Intelligence Squadron, Little Rock AFB, Arkansas. In March 2015,

Col. Lipscomb transferred to the A1/Deputy Director of Staff-Air, Joint Force Headquarters, Camp Robinson.

On June 24, 2018, Col. Lipscomb was promoted to the rank of Colonel, and served as the Director of Staff in the Arkansas Air National Guard. Col. Lipscomb transferred back to the 189th Airlift Wing in April 2019 as the Mission Support Group Commander, Little Rock AFB, Arkansas. On September 11, 2022, Col. Lipscomb became the Deputy Commander second in charge of the 189th Airlift Wing.

Col. Lipscomb's military education includes Squadron Officer School, Air Command and Staff College, and the U.S. Air Force Air War College.

Chief Warrant Officer Four
Edith J. (Sandy) Milligan

First Female to Graduate from the
Warrant Officer Candidate School

CW4 Edith (Sandy) J. Milligan is a native of Tennessee and was born in 1943. She graduated from University of Arkansas at Pine Bluff in 1975 with a degree in Business Administration. She enlisted in the Arkansas Army National Guard on July 8, 1976.

CW4 Milligan began her military career as a Private First Class in the Headquarters and Headquarters Detachment of the 455th Transportation Battalion in Pine Bluff, Arkansas. She attended Basic Training in January of 1977, and completed Advanced Individual Training to obtain her 71B10 Military Occupational Specialist (MOS) and rank of Specialist (E4). She served as a Clerk and Dispatch Specialist with 455th Transportation and attained the rank of Sergeant until 1980 when she was honorably discharged from the Arkansas Army National Guard (AR ARNG).

She reentered the AR ARNG in 1986 with the goal of becoming a Warrant Officer. In 1989, she became the first female in the AR ARNG to graduate from the Reserve Component Warrant Officer Candidate School. She was appointed a Warrant Office One in August 1989, and served as a Military Personnel Technician with the State Area Command, Headquarters Arkansas Army National Guard.

CW4 Milligan was instrumental in establishing family readiness programs for the entire state during Operation Desert Shield/Desert Storm. She designed, edited, and printed, "What About Us", Family Support publication for 455th Transportation Battalion. CW4 Milligan also designed and edited the Family Support Program publication for the Arkansas Air and Army National Guard. She also worked as Military Personnel Technician in 2-114th Aviation, Det 1, 87th Troop Command and National Guard Marksmanship Training Center prior to her retirement in 2003.

In addition, to the Warrant Officer Candidate School, CW4 Milligan has completed numerous military schools to include Warrant Officer Advance Course and Warrant Officer Staff Course. She received numerous awards and service medals to recognize her incredible service to include the Army Commendation Medal.

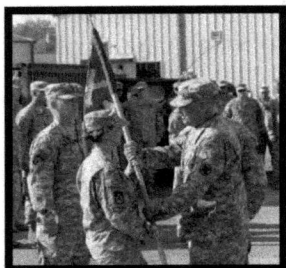

Major Clara R. Moser

First Female Field Artillery Officer in the Arkansas Army National Guard

First Female Company Level Commander of a Field Artillery Firing Battery in the Arkansas Army National Guard

Major (MAJ) Clara Moser was born November 8, 1988, in Oklahoma City and graduated from West Monroe High School, West Monroe, Louisiana in 2007. MAJ Moser earned a Bachelor of Arts in General Studies with a focus in Early Childhood Education from Arkansas Tech University in 2012. MAJ Moser also earned a Master of Arts in Marriage and Family Therapy from Amridge University in 2016.

MAJ Clara Moser enlisted in the Louisiana Army National Guard (LA ARNG) as a 25B on January 12, 2006, as a Private First Class (PFC/E3) during her junior year of high school. She attended Basic Combat Training the summer between her junior and senior year of high school. Upon graduation in 2007, she attended her Advanced Individual Training (AIT) at Fort Gordon, Georgia and graduated in October 2007. MAJ Moser volunteered to deploy with the LA ARNG in support of Operation Iraqi Freedom in November of 2007, and began pre-mobilization training in January 2008. At the conclusion of her OIF deployment, MAJ Moser interstate transferred to the Arkansas Army National Guard and joined the 1-206th FA as a Specialist (E4). She promoted to Sergeant (E5) December 8, 2009, at Headquarters and Headquarters Company, 39th Brigade Support Battalion (BSB).

In spring 2010, MAJ Moser was selected for Officer Candidate School and attended the 2010 summer accelerated program. She graduated class 53 as class honor graduate, receiving the Erickson Trophy and

High Physical Test Awards, and commissioned September 25, 2010. MAJ Moser was assigned as a platoon leader with Alpha Company, 39th BSB September 2010 followed by assignment as the executive officer of A Co, 39th BSB in June 2011. MAJ Moser attend Ordnance Basic Officer Leader Course (OD BOLC), at then, Fort Lee, Virginia, and graduated November 2011. While attending OD BOLC, MAJ Moser planned and participated in the German Armed Forces Proficiency Badge Competition, earning the gold badge and the German Command Coin. Upon graduation MAJ Moser continued as the executive officer for A Co, 39th BSB and participated in the National Training Center (NTC) rotation at Fort Irwin, California in preparation for deployment to Afghanistan (off ramped). In October 2012, MAJ Moser was selected to attend the active component Combined Logistics Captains Career Course (CLC3) at Fort Lee, Virginia, graduating in March 2013. While attending CLC3, MAJ Moser completed Level I and Level II Modern Army Combatives Program Certifications.

In July 2013, MAJ Moser was selected as Aide-de-Camp (ADC) for the AR ARNG Land Component Commander and served as the ADC for a year. July 2014, she transferred to the 1-206th FA as the Battalion S4/Logistics Officer in preparation for a transition to the Field Artillery Branch. MAJ Moser enrolled in the Field Artillery Captains Career Course and graduated December 2014.

On January 11, 2015, MAJ Moser became the first female Field Artillery Officer for the Arkansas Army National Guard. On July 1, 2015, MAJ Moser took command of Alpha Battery, 1-142nd Multiple Launch Rocket System (MLRS), 142nd Field Artillery Brigade as the first female Firing Battery Commander in Arkansas. This was a position previously excluded for females prior to 2012. Upon completion of command, MAJ Moser was selected to deploy as the executive officer to Chief of Staff Kosovo Forces from September 2016 to September 2017. Following this assignment, MAJ Moser was assigned as the Battalion Training Officer/Assistant S3 Officer for 777th Aviation Support Battalion from September 2017 to August 2019. In

June 2019, MAJ Moser was selected as the state and the national General Douglas MacArthur Leadership Award recipient.

In August 2019, MAJ Moser was assigned as the Support Operations Officer for the 217th Brigade Support Battalion in support of the 142nd FAB. After a successful tour, MAJ Moser was selected as the 871st Troop Command Executive/Administrative Officer in August 2020. While assigned as the 871st TC EO, she completed Command and General Staff College Common Core (ILE) June 2021. MAJ Moser was then selected as the Arkansas National Guard J34/Force Protection Officer at the Directorate of Military Support (DOMS) from August 2021 to October 2022. Currently, MAJ Moser holds her second command with the 119th Mobile Public Affairs Detachment (MPAD). While in command, she completed Command and General Staff College Advanced Operations Course (AOC) January 2023, and the Joint Operations Center Training Course June 2023.

MAJ Moser has received numerous awards and decorations to include the Defense Meritorious Service Medal, Meritorious Service Medal (2), Army Commendation Medal (6), Army Achievement Medal (3), Army Good Conduct Medal, Army Reserve Components Achievement Medal (2), National Defense Service Medal, Armed Forces Expeditionary Medal, Military Outstanding Volunteer Service Medal, Iraqi Campaign Medal with Campaign Star, Global War on Terrorism Medal, Armed Forces Reserve Medal with Bronze Hourglass and 2 "M" Device, Army Service Ribbon, Overseas Service Ribbon with Bronze Star Device, NATO Service Ribbon, Meritorious Unit Citation, General Douglas MacArthur Leadership Award, German Armed Proficiency Badge (Gold), Arkansas Service Ribbon with diamond, and Louisiana War Cross Ribbon.

MAJ Moser is married to Casey, and they have 5 children, Dylan (14), Tyler (12), Olivia (18 months), and twins John and Adelin (newborn).

Major General Betty L Mullis

First Female Pilot
Arkansas Air National Guard

Major General (Maj. Gen.) Betty L. Mullis was born in St. Francis, Kansas. She graduated from The University of Northern Colorado in 1970 earning a Bachelor of Science Degree in Biological Sciences. In 1982, she earned her Master's Degree in Operations Management from The University of Arkansas.

Maj. Gen. Mullis joined the Air Force and graduated from Officer Training School in 1972. From July 1972 to September 1972, she was a student at the Administrative Management and Executive Officer School in Keesler AFB, Mississippi. Additional military education completed includes Squadron Officer School by correspondence and Air Command and Staff College in 1981. She also completed Air War College in 1994.

From September 1972 to September 1977, Brig. Gen. Mullis served in an active-duty role for the 314th Tactical Airlift Wing at the Little Rock AFB.

Maj. Gen. Mullis joined the 189th in September 1977 and served as a Public Affairs Officer in the Arkansas Air National Guard at the Little Rock Airforce Base. In 1979 and 1980, Maj. Gen. Mullis completed undergraduate pilot training at Reese AFB, Texas and KC-135E Combat Crew Training School at Castle AFB, California, making her the first female pilot in the Arkansas Air National Guard, and the third in the United States. Additionally, Maj. Gen. Mullis was a flight supervisor and C-130E instructor, 154th Tactical Airlift

Training Squadron, Arkansas Air National Guard, Little Rock AFB, Arkansas.

In 1988, after spending 11 years in the Arkansas Air National Guard, Brig. Gen. Mullis transitioned to the Air Force Reserve. From November 1993 to February 1995, she was the 336th Air Refueling Squadron Commander, March AFB, California. In 1995, she served as the special assistant to the Commander, 452nd Air Mobility Wing, March AFB, California. She served as Commander of 940th Air Refueling Wing at McClellan AFB, California from 1996 to 1998 and Mobilization Assistant to the Commandant at Air War College, Maxwell AFB, Alabama from April 1998 to June 2000.

In June 2000, she was promoted to Brigadier General, then on September 1, 2002, she was promoted to Major General. For the next 4 years, she served as the mobilization assistant to the Director of Operations and assistant to the Commander, Headquarters Air Education and Training Command at Randolph AFB, Texas. In her last position held, Maj. Gen. Mullis served as Director, Reserve Readiness, Joint Reserve Forces (J9), and mobilization assistant to the Deputy Director of the Defense Logistics Agency, Fort Belvoir, Virginia.

Maj. Gen. Mullis retired from the military on September 1, 2005. In her civilian career, Maj. Gen. Mullis was an airline pilot. In her military career, she was a command pilot with more than 4,900 flying hours in military aircraft with the following aircrafts flown: KC-135A, KC-135E, C-130E, C141B, T-38 and T-37. She participated in worldwide air refueling and airlift operations including Desert Storm, Provide Hope and Joint Endeavor. She was the Air Force Reserve Military Representative to the Defense Advisory Committee on Women in the Services from 1995 to 1997, and she served on the Reserve Forces Policy Board as well as the Air Reserve Forces Policy Committee.

She was involved in the following professional memberships and associations: Air Force Association, Women in Aviation, International Airlift/Tanker Association, Women Military Aviators Lifetime member, Reserve Officers Association Lifetime member and Order of Daedalians.

Her Major awards and decorations include: Distinguished Service Medal, Legion of Merit, Meritorious Service Medal with oak leaf cluster, Air Medal, Aerial Achievement Medal, Air Force Commendation Medal with oak leaf cluster, Air Force Achievement Medal Air Force Outstanding Unit Award with "V" device and four oak leaf clusters, Combat Readiness Medal with four oak leaf clusters, National Defense Service Medal with bronze star, Southwest Asia Service Medal with two bronze stars, Armed

Forces Service Medal, Air Force, Longevity Award with silver oak leaf clusters, Armed Forces Reserve Medal, Small Arms Marksmanship Ribbon with bronze star, Air Force Training Ribbon and Kuwait Liberation Medal (Kingdom of Saudi Arabia).

Captain Jamie R. Newton

First Federally Recognized Female Infantry Officer Arkansas Army National Guard

Captain (CPT) Jamie Newton was born 1987 in Springdale, Arkansas and graduated from Arkansas State University in 2009 with a Bachelor's Degree in General Science. In 2011, she earned a second Bachelor's Degree in Dietetics and Nutrition and Master's Degree in Dietetics and Nutrition in 2015, both from the University of Central Arkansas. Captain Newton is also a licensed Dietitian through the State of Arkansas.

CPT Newton enlisted in the Arkansas Army National Guard on June 25, 2013, as a 09S assigned to the 216th MP Company. She went on to go to Officer Candidate School and in 2017, she commissioned as a 70B, Medical Officer where she was assigned to 39th BSB Charlie Med. CPT Newton spent time as the Treatment Platoon Leader and Executive Officer. In July 2020, CPT Newton was assigned to 39th IBCT 2/153rd IN BN, Charlie Company as a Platoon Leader of 1st platoon followed by serving as the Executive Officer for Charlie Company. CPT Newton was assigned as the Assistant S3/Plans Officer for 2/153rd IN BN January 2022. On July 17, 2022, CPT Newton because the first Federally Recognized Female Infantry Officer in the Arkansas Army National Guard.

CPT Newton is a graduate of Officer Candidate School, Medical Basic Officer Leadership Course, and Maneuver Captain Career Course. CPT Newton has numerous personal accomplishments throughout her career including being awarded the Leadership Award in OCS class 60 in 2017, completing the Master Fitness Trainer program in 2017, graduating Top 10% of her class at the Air Assault course in 2019, completing the Arkansas Pre-Ranger Program in 2021 and graduating from Rappel Master school in 2022. She is also a member of the "All Guard Marathon Team" and the "All Guard Endurance Team."

Captain Newton has also received many awards and decorations including the Meritorious Service Medal, the Army Commendation Medal, the Army Achievement Medal with one Oak Leaf Clusters, National Defense Service Medal, and Army Service Ribbon.

CPT Newton has two children, CharliAnne (8) and Carver (6).

Colonel Sarah O'Banion

First Female Maintenance Group Commander, 189th Airlift Wing, Arkansas Air National Guard

Colonel (Col.) Sarah O'Banion was born and raised in Houston, Texas. She graduated from J. Frank Dobie High School in 1998, and as a military spouse, moved to her husband Thomas' first duty station, Naval Station Everett, Washington, where he served as a Boatswains mate on board the USS Abraham Lincoln. She earned a Bachelor of Science Degree in Mathematics from Seattle Pacific University and received her commission through the University of Washington's Detachment 910 ROTC Program in 2002. Col. O'Banion graduated from the University of Central Arkansas with a Master's Degree in Teaching in 2010.

Col. O'Banion attended Joint Undergraduate Specialized Navigator training in San Antonio, Texas and earned her wings in 2003. After completing C-130 training, her next duty assignment Yokota Air Base, Tokyo, Japan, where she participated in Operations Unified Assistance, Iraqi Freedom, and Enduring Freedom. During this 2004-2007 assignment, she served as a Training Officer, Scheduler, Executive Officer, and Instructor.

Col. O'Banion's family arrived in Little Rock in 2007, where she served with the 53rd and 62nd Airlift Squadrons as a Formal Training Unit Instructor and Team Little Rock Current Operations Scheduler. In 2009, Col. O'Banion transferred to the Arkansas Air National Guard as a Formal Training Unit Instructor in the 154th Training Squadron and served as the wing's Protocol Officer.

In October 2011, Col. O'Banion transferred to the National Guard Bureau where she became the Future Operations Cell Director and Joint Homeland Defense Action Officer for the J3/7 Directorate. She led the National Guard Coordination Center through Superstorm Sandy ensuring synchronized efforts between U.S. Northern Command, the National Guard, Governmental and Civilian agencies.

In 2014, Col. O'Banion returned to the 189th Airlift Wing and has served in the roles of Assistant Navigator Flight Chief, Director of Operations of the 189th Operations Support Squadron, 189th Airlift Wing Chief of Safety and 189th Maintenance Squadron Commander. Since December 2022, Col. O'Banion has served as the first female Commander of the 189th Maintenance Group, overseeing the health of the wing's C-130 fleet.

Col. O'Banion's military education includes Squadron Officer School, Air Command and Staff College, U.S. Air Force Air War College, Joint Combined Warfighting School, and the Reserve National Security Course.

Chief Warrant Officer Three (CW3) Amelia (Dawson) Penn

First Female Pilot in Command, Arkansas Army National Guard

Chief Warrant Officer Three (CW3) Amelia Penn entered service when she enlisted in the Arkansas Army National Guard on August 9, 1990, between her Junior and Senior year of high school. Having participated in the Junior ROTC program at Benton High School, she enlisted as a Private First Class (E3) and was assigned to Bravo Company, 212th Signal Battalion as a Mobile Subscriber Equipment Operator (31F10). Upon completion of Benton High School in 1991, she shipped out for Basic Training at Fort Jackson, South Carolina and then Advanced Individual Training (AIT) at Fort Gordon, Georgia. Upon completion of training, she returned to Arkansas and Bravo company while concurrently enrolling at Henderson State University for her first semester of college. In 1995, Amy transferred to 1st of the 114th (1-114th) Aviation Battalion located at Camp Joseph T Robinson, North Little Rock, Arkansas with the ambition to be an Army Aviator. She was approved by a selection board and soon departed for Warrant Officer Candidate School and Army Aviation Initial Entry Rotary Wing (IERW) School for training as a helicopter pilot. She completed IERW August 1997. Over the next few years, she became qualified to fly both the UH-1 Huey and UH-60 Black Hawk helicopters. On April 4, 2006, CW3 Penn was called to active duty and deployed to Iraq with C-Company, 1-185th Aviation in support of Operation Iraqi Freedom. She flew over 500 combat hours over the year she was stationed at Camp Anaconda, Balad Iraq.

After returning home she enrolled in the University of Arkansas at Little Rock School of Nursing the fall of 2007, and graduated

December of 2009 as a Registered Nurse with an Associates of Science in Nursing.

In 2008, Amy received the designation Pilot in Command (PIC); the first female Arkansas Army Aviator to do so.

In April 2010, she was once again called to active duty and deployed to Camp Bondsteel, Kosovo with F Company 2/238th Aviation serving as a Medevac pilot and Aviation Safety Officer in support of the 13th rotation of Kosovo Forces (KFOR-13). While deployed she enrolled in the Nursing Bachelor Completion program through on-line correspondence at the University of Arkansas at Little Rock.

Once home, she pursued her nursing career and began work at the Little Rock VA in August 2011. She completed her Bachelor of Science in Nursing December 19, 2015.

CW3 Penn retired from military service on April 30, 2015, with 24 years of service.

Today, Amy resides in Little Rock with husband MG Kendall Penn. They enjoy traveling and backpacking and serving at their church home, New Life Church. She continues to work at the Little Rock VA where cares for our nation's heroes, which she considers the most rewarding work of her life.

Among her awards are the Meritorious Service Ribbon, Army Air Medal, Army Commendation Medal, Army Achievement Medal with Oakleaf Cluster, Iraqi Campaign Medal with two Campaign Stars and the Senior Aviator Badge. In her civilian career as a Registered Nurse, she is a Certified Oncology nurse. She was also recognized with the Daisy Award for excellence in Nursing November 2019, and was selected as an Arkansas Top 100 Nurses for 2020.

First Seargent
Heather L. Peters

First Female First Seargent
of the 106th Army Band

First Seargent (1SG) Heather Peters was born in Fort Smith, Arkansas, and graduated from Bryant High School in 2002. She earned her Bachelor's Degree in Music Education in May 2006 from Arkansas Tech University. She also earned her Master's Degree in Library Media and Information Sciences in 2012 from the University of Central Arkansas.

1SG Heather Peters enlisted in the Arkansas Army National Guard on October 24, 2002, as a flute player in the 106th Army Band. Since her enlistment, her assignments include Instrumentalist, Senior Instrumentalist, Assistant Team Leader, Team Leader, and Public Affairs Noncommissioned Officer in Charge.

1SG Peters served as acting 1SG for the 119th Mobile Public Affairs Detachment from December 2020 to March 2021. She took responsibility of the 106th Army Band in September 2021, cementing her as the first female First Sergeant for the 106th Army Band. 1SG Peters laterally transferred back to take responsibility of the 119th Mobile Public Affairs Detachment as the First Seargent in January 2023.

1SG Peters has 21 years of service in the National Guard. She has completed Basic Combat Training (2003), Primary Leader Development Course (2004), Basic Noncommissioned Officer Course, Phase 1 (2009), Advanced Leader Course (2011), Senior Leader Course (2017), and graduated on the Commandant's List for Master Leader Course on April 2, 2021.

1SG Peters awards include the Army Commendation Medal (7), Army Achievement Medal (3), Army Good Conduct Medal, Reserve Components Achievement Medal (6), National Defense Service Medal, Armed Forces Reserve Medal, NCO Professional Development Ribbon (4), Army Service Ribbon, and the Arkansas Service Ribbon (3).

She and her husband, Jason, reside in Springdale where she works as a Library Media Specialist at Rogers High School in her 17th year in education. Together they have one daughter, Valentine (4) and one son, Dorian (1).

Specialist Shray A. Ricker

First Female in the Arkansas Army National Guard to Graduate From 12B Combat Engineer Reclassification Course

Specialist (SPC) Shray Ricker was born in Paragould, Arkansas. She grew up in Corning, Arkansas and graduated from Corning High School in 2014. SPC Ricker joined the Arkansas Army National Guard on April 17, 2014, one month before graduating high school.

SPC Ricker completed Basic Combat Training at Fort Leonard Wood, Missouri and Advanced Individual Training at Fort Lee, Virginia in 2015. SPC Ricker started her Army career as a Small Arms and Artillery Specialist (91F) assigned to the Forward Support Company, 875th Engineer Battalion in Jonesboro, Arkansas.

In March 2016, she completed the Combat Engineer Reclassification Course, awarding her the 12B MOS, a combat engineer. This made her the first female in the Arkansas Army National Guard to graduate from the 12B Combat Engineer Reclassification Course. This MOS was restricted to females until 2014. SPC Ricker was then transferred to the 1036th Sapper Company of the 875th Battalion located in Jonesboro. SPC Ricker was the only female in the 1036th unit for at least one year.

SPC Ricker continued her career as a 12B with the 1036th Sapper Company until she was honorably discharged April 16, 2020. While with the 1036th, SPC Ricker completed various trainings and was awarded the Army Achievement Medal (AAM) for exceptional performance of duty.

Shray Ricker is currently living in Trenton, Florida with her two children and is a daycare teacher. Shray Ricker is a Boy Scouts of America (BSA) leader in the local troop. Her hobbies include kayaking and making many outdoor memories with her children.

Colonel Alicia "Cissy" Rucker

First Female in the Arkansas Army National Guard to Attend and Graduate the U.S. Army Rotary Wing School

First Female State Public Affairs Officer

First Female Inducted into the Arkansas Military Academy OCS Hall of Fame Arkansas Army National Guard

Colonel (COL) Alicia "Cissy" Rucker was born in Little Rock, Arkansas. She graduated from Sylvan High School in 1967, and received a Bachelor of Art in Sociology from the University of Arkansas at Little Rock in 1972. She received a Master's Degree in Marketing from Webster University in 1990.

COL Rucker's began her stellar military career on December 29, 1975, when she enlisted in the 176th Public Affairs Detachment (PAD), Arkansas Army National Guard, Camp Robinson, Arkansas. As a member of the 176th Public Affairs Detachment, she served as a photographer and writer. Her enlistment was under the Civilian Acquired Skills Program (CASP) so basic training was two weeks at Fort McClellan, Alabama. Due to her education degree and related civilian employment, COL Rucker was not required to attend Advanced Individual Training (AIT).

In 1976, COL Rucker attended Officer Candidate School (OCS) at the Arkansas Military Academy. On May 13, 1977, she completed the OCS Program and received her commissioned as 2nd Lieutenant,

Adjutant Generals Corps. She was later branch transferred to the Signal Corps in order to apply for U.S. Army Rotary Flight Training. On May 26, 1981, COL Rucker was the first female from the Arkansas Army National Guard to attend the U.S. Army Rotary Wing Course and the first female Class Leader at Fort Rucker, Alabama. On February 10, 1982, she completed the U.S. Army Rotary Wing Course and became the first female UH-1 Huey Helicopter Pilot in the history of the Arkansas Army National Guard. In addition to flying the UH-1 Huey Helicopter, she also flew the UH-60 Blackhawk Helicopter.

COL Rucker held a variety of command and staff assignments in three primary career fields: Public Affairs, Aviation and Surface Maintenance. In 1990 and 1991, she took a Public Affairs Team to Saudi Arabia, Kuwait, Iraq, England, and Germany in support of Operations Desert Shield and Desert Storm. In 1990, she was the first female State Public Affairs Officer. She was the first female in this role. Her other assignments include Public Information Officer, Headquarters, Arkansas National Guard, Pilot Aircraft Command, STARC (-), Arkansas Army National Guard, Commander, 176th Public Affairs Detachment, Little Rock, Liaison Officer, Headquarters and Headquarters Detachment (HHD), 2nd Battalion 114th Aviation Battalion, Camp Robinson, S2/S3, HHD, 2nd Battalion, 114th Aviation, Camp Robinson, Executive Officer, HHD, 2nd Battalion, 114th Aviation, Maintenance Manager, STARC (-), Commander, 1/ 87th Troop Command, North Little Rock, Commander Robinson Army Airfield, Camp Robinson, State Aviation Officer and State Maintenance Officer.

Her military education includes the Adjutant General Officer Basic Course, Defense Information Officer Course, Officer Rotary Wing Aviation Course; Signal Officer Advanced Course, Command Information Officer Course, Command and General Staff Officer Course, Rotary Wing Refresher Course, Maintenance Managers Course, Aviation Executive Management Course, Pre-Command Course, UH-60 Blackhawk Qualification Course, Recruiting and Retention Course and the Army Community of Excellence Course.

COL Rucker's career was marked with distinction through the receipt of the following awards, decorations and honors to include the Legion of Merit Medal, Meritorious Service Medal, Joint Service Commendation Medal, Army Commendation Medal, Army Achievement Medal, Army Reserve Components Achievement Medal, National Defense Medal, Southwest Asia Service Medal, Humanitarian Service Medal, Armed Forces Reserve Medal, Army Service Ribbon, Army Reserve Component Training Ribbon, Army Aviator Badge, Senior Army Aviator Badge, Arkansas Distinguished Service Ribbon, Arkansas Service Ribbon and the Arkansas Recruiting Ribbon. In 2012, COL Rucker became the first female in the Arkansas Army National Guard inducted into the Arkansas Military Academy Officer Candidate School (OCS) Hall of Fame.

On May 31, 2009, COL Rucker retired with over 33 years of outstanding military service. After retirement, COL Rucker was appointed as the first female Director of the Arkansas Department of Veterans Affairs by Governor Mike Beebe. She also served as Deputy Director of Arkansas Career Education. Her affiliations include Former Member, Hot Springs Rehabilitation Center Hospital Boar, Volunteer, Arkansas Children's Hospital and University of Arkansas Medical Sciences; Member Hot Springs National Park Rotary Club, Sigma Delta Chi (Society of Professional Journalists), Member, Pulaski Heights United Methodist Church, Member, National Guard Associations of Arkansas and the United States, Member, Employer Support of the Guard and Reserve Committee, Member, Women's International Helicopter Pilots Association, Member, Arkansas "99s", Member, Army Aviation Association of America, Former Member, Board of Directors, Arkansas National Guard Museum and Former Member, State Operated Comprehensive Rehabilitation Centers Consortium.

COL Rucker and her husband COL Steve Rucker are both retired and reside in Little Rock.

Colonel Edith "Cory" Sailor

First Female Construction & Facility Management Officer (CFMO/DCSEN), Arkansas Army National Guard

COL Cory Sailor began her military career when she commissioned as a Second Lieutenant, Military Police upon graduation with a Bachelor of Fine Arts Degree in Graphic Design and completion of the Reserve Officer Training Corps at the University of Memphis on May 9, 1992.

She entered the Arkansas National Guard and transitioned to the Medical Service Corps to serve as a platoon leader for the 216th Medical Company (Ground Ambulance) in Lake Village, Arkansas. She has served in a variety of command and staff assignments throughout her career to include commander of 2nd Detachment, 296th Medical Company. Deploying in support of Operation Joint Guard, and responsible for the ground evacuation throughout Hungary, Croatia, and Bosnia. Upon returning, she took command of the 296th Medical Company, later serving as the S1 and XO for the 212th Signal Battalion; and S4 for the 87th Troop Command. She then returned to the 212th Signal Battalion, as the executive and administrative officer, where she coordinated and managed the deactivation of the unit and casing the colors.

In 2007, she deployed to Iraq as the S4 for 871st Troop Command. Upon return, she was assigned as the G4 logistics management branch chief for Joint Force Headquarters. She commanded the 39th Brigade Support Battalion between 2011 and 2014, after which, she served as the brigade executive officer for 87th Troop Command, while continuing to work full-time as the Director of Property and Fiscal Office.

142

COL Sailor served as the Deputy Chief of Staff, Logistics (G4) for six years where she was awarded the Legion of Merit. In 2020 she assumed brigade command of the 87th Troop Command. In 2022, she was assigned as the Construction & Facility Management Officer/Deputy Chief of Staff, Engineering (G9) and it is in this role that COL Sailor became the first female to hold this position.

COL Sailor is a 2015 graduate of the U.S. Army War College.

Colonel Alice K. Sanders

**First Female Commander, 189th
Logistics Squadron**

**First Female Commander, 189th
Mission Support Group
Arkansas Air National Guard**

Colonel (Col.) Alice K. Sanders was born in Toledo, Ohio and spent her early years in Ohio and New Jersey. She graduated from high school in Maumee, Ohio in 1972. She received her Bachelor of Science Liberal Science Degree from Excelsior College of Albany, New York in 2001.

Col. Sanders enlisted in the U.S. Air Force in 1974 as a stenographer with the 316th Tactical Airlift Wing, Langley Air Force Base, Virginia. While serving in this role, she recalled her First Sergeant telling her that he didn't think that women serving in the military should have children. At this time, she "traded in the military for motherhood." Currently Col. Sanders has children and adorable grandchildren, proving the First Sergeant wrong.

Col. Sanders enlisted in the Arkansas Air National Guard in 1978 as an Administrative Specialist in the 189th Resource Management Squadron at Little Rock AFB. Her first goal was to get a full-time job. She asked her recruiter, Master Sergeant Buddy Burns, how to do that and he responded, "work hard, stay out of trouble, and let people know what [you] want."

Col. Sanders attained the rank of Technical Sergeant before receiving a commission. She completed the Academy of Military Science at McGhee-Tyson Air National Guard Base, Tennessee and was commissioned as a Second Lieutenant in 1983.

After receiving her commission as a traditional guardsman, Col. Sanders was assigned to the 189th Mission Support Squadron where she served as the Executive Support Officer. She later accomplished her goal of receiving a full-time position in 1983.

In addition to being the first female Colonel in the 189th and the Arkansas Air National Guard, Colonel Sanders' 32+ military career has showcased several other notable first female accomplishments:

- April 1988 - November 1989: First female Chief of Disaster Preparedness Branch, 189th Mission Support Squadron, Arkansas Air National Guard
- November 1991 - September 1997: First female Chief of Supply, 189th Logistics Squadron, Arkansas Air National Guard
- September 1997 - January 2003: First female Commander, 189th Logistics Squadron, Arkansas Air National Guard
- January 2003 - October 2007: First female Commander, 189th Mission Support Group, Arkansas Air National Guard
- January 30, 2003: First female Colonel (0-6) in Arkansas Air National Guard
- November 2007 - January 2010: First female Vice Wing Commander, 189th Airlift Wing, Arkansas Air National Guard

Col. Sanders said her military career accomplishments while serving in the Arkansas Air National Guard were often met without female role models. She said, "There wasn't always a female role model there for me, it was kind of lonely; we didn't have people to talk to."

Col. Sanders awards and decorations include, but are not limited to, the Meritorious Service Medal, the Air Force Commendation Medal, the Air Force Achievement Medal with one oak leaf cluster, the Air Force Outstanding Unit Award with two oak leaf clusters, the National Defense Service Medal with one device, and the Armed Forces Reserve Medal.

CW4 Dorothy Lee Sealy

First Female Warrant Officer, 39th Infantry Brigade

Chief Warrant Officer Four (CW4) Dorothy Sealy was born in Malvern, Arkansas and attended Malvern High School and Ouachita Vo-Tech. After answering an advertisement from *The Daily Record*, on June 29, 1973, at the age of 30 she raised her hand and became a member of the Arkansas Army National Guard. She was the third female in the state to enlist after Helen Nichols and Martha Jane Kasiah enlisted in February of 1973. These three ladies were true trailblazers.

Headquarters and Headquarters Company (HHC), 212th Signal Battalion Operations (S3) Section became then Private Sealy's first military home. In October 1973, she flew to Anniston, Alabama, Fort McClellan, Women's Army Corps Training Center. SSG Bess became her drill sergeant. She quickly realized that her training in the Malvern High School band prepared her how to march. She became friends with Eleanor from Richmond, Virginia and Paulette from Chicago, Illinois and they all remained friends for over fifty years. She attended Advanced Individual Training (AIT) in Fort Ord, California and received an advance promotion to Private First Class (E3).

Starting her military career at age of 30, with three children, came with many challenges. She joined the Arkansas Army National Guard for the many opportunities. It was a chance to earn extra money and a chance to serve one's country. The mid 1970's was the beginning of a transformational time for the National Guard. During her first drill while standing in formation, she noticed a few men wearing wigs to cover their long hair. After that same formation, the

147

First Sergeant took her aside and said, "This is a man's Army, and if you want to be a part you have to work harder, study harder than the men, I am not saying it's fair or right, that's just how it is." She took his earnest advice and did just that.

In 1975, she served as a recruiter for Colonel Bill Cook, Commander of the Arkansas Recruiting and Retention battalion. In 1976, she became a Civil Service employee and a member of HHC, 1st of the 153rd Infantry Battalion. She was proud to be a member of an Infantry unit. She served with the 39th Infantry Brigade for over 10 years, obtaining the rank of Sergeant First Class (E7) prior to her appointment as a Warrant Officer. During this time, she also served as a member of the first Governor's Color Guard. This came with numerous unique experiences, for example, she was able to be at the Razorback games as well as being able to stand behind Country Music star Johnny and June Cash.

CW4 Sealy has experienced many firsts in her career. In October 1980, she was the second female in the state to receive a direct commission to Warrant Officer and the first female Warrant Officer in the 39th Infantry Brigade. For her, this topped the list of career achievements. She also maintained her service as dual-status military member with both military and civil service positions. As a civil servant she was a human resource specialist and worked for CW4 Bennie Wilson at the Camp Robinson Human Resource Office (HRO). She was honored to serve there for many years, and it led to her civilian promotion to GS-11. She transferred to the Installation Support Unit at Camp Robinson in July of 1988 to become the first female Personnel Officer in that unit. It was another adventure for her career.

CW4 Sealy spent 23 years in the Civil Service and 29 years in the military. She states that she could not have done it without the love, support and encouragement from her mom, stepfather and all eight of her brothers and sisters. It has been decades since her retirement, and she fondly recalls memories of the wonderful organization called the Arkansas Army National Guard. CW4 Sealy is extremely grateful to the many people that gave her a chance to advance her career and wishes to thank all who had faith in her to get the job done. All her military friends mean so much to her.

Colonel Mary Frances "Frankie" Sears

First Army National Guard Female to Graduate from the U.S. Army War College

First Arkansas Army National Guard Female to attend the U.S. Army War College

First Female President of National Guard Association of Arkansas and any National Guard Association in the United States

Colonel (COL) Mary Frances "Frankie" Sears was born on June 10, 1937. She was the first-born child of Ernest Anthony "Bud" Wallace and Vallye Genevia Stacy Wallace. Two more children followed a boy, Ronald Ermest, and a girl Patricia Ann. All three children were born at home with the assistance of an untrained midwife. After each birth, the doctor arrived sometime later to check out the new arrival!

She graduated from Malvern High School on a Friday night in May of 1955, and started nursing school at Arkansas Baptist Hospital School of Nursing the following Monday. The school is now known as Baptist Health College. This was a three-year diploma program.

On March 12, 1976, she received a direct commission as a First Lieutenant, assigned to the 148th Evacuation Hospital located at Ricks Armory in Little Rock. She was assigned as an operating room nurse. By this time, she had 18 years' experience as a Registered Nurse (RN). A few months later she was reassigned as the Head Nurse of the Operating Room.

In the fall of 1976, COL Sears was nominated/selected/told, that she was the 148th member to the Board of Directors National Guard Association of Arkansas (NGAA). Having no idea what this consisted of, she attended her first meeting on a Saturday morning of Drill weekend. She was the only female in the room of these Air and Army Guard Majors and grades above that all out ranked a 1st Lieutenant.

After serving on the Board of Directors for four years, several members began talking to COL Sears about seeking the office of President. She agreed to having her name submitted to the nominating committee. She had been promoted to Captain. It was also agreed upon should the nominating committee not select her, that she would seek the office by "running from the floor." The nominating committee did not select her as the preferred candidate.

At the board meeting that day COL Sears announced that she would be seeking the office of president by being nominated from the floor of the conference. This was done so the planning committee would have ballots ready to distribute to the membership. After the board meeting that day one of the board members attempted to get her to change her mind. Basically, telling her there would be time for her later. Her response was, "Are you trying to tell me it is not my turn?"

The next three to four months COL Sears visited Air and Army Guard units around the state to introduce herself and explain why she was seeking the office of president and asking for their vote. During the NGAA General Conference in the spring of 1980, she was elected 2nd Vice-president. The normal order of succession to the presidency was to serve a year as 2nd Vice, then a year as 1st Vice, then assume the presidency. So, in the spring of 1983, the Major assumed the Office of President of the National Guard Association of Arkansas, making her the first female to be elected President of any National Guard Association in the United States.

At this time, NGAA had not had a full-time person that attended to the business of the association. This situation was very worrisome to COL Sears because there was a lot of money laying around without a guardian. These concerns of COL Sears led to NGAA hiring a full-time secretary and then progressed to hiring a full-time Executive Director to oversee the operation of the association.

From 1976 through 1978, COL Sears attended St. Vincent Infirmary School of Nurse Anesthesia. Her assignment in the 148th change to anesthesia. COL Sears was attending night school at University of Arkansas at Little Rock and Park College (Little Rock Air Force Base Campus) and graduated in May 1988 from Park College with a Bachelor of Science in Social Psychology.

During the summer of 1990, COL Sears was selected to attend the United States Army War College Corresponding Studies Course, a two-year course of study. She was the first female in the Arkansas National Guard to attend the United States Army War College. She was the 2nd Army Guard female to be selected to attend the course. During her second year, just prior to graduation the Army National Guard Advisor to the War College notified her that she would be the first National Guard female to graduate from the War College. The other female that was selected to attend had transferred to the Army Reserve prior to her graduation.

In1992, COL Sears was assigned as Chief Nurse of 148th Evac. Hospital. Then in 1996, she was assigned as Chief Nurse STARC (-). In June 1997, COL Sears retired with the rank of Colonel.

All throughout her years in the Army Guard, she was a constant reminder to her male counterparts that women were present. When they prayed to protect the service men in harm's way, she would simply add in an audible voice "and the women." In 1996, she called the Adjutants General's office and the male voice said, "Command Sergent Major _____, How may I help you SIR?" COL Sears stopped breathing for a moment. He then said, "Hello, Hello." Her response to him was, "Command Sergent Major, do not answer the phone that way anymore, there are women in your man's army now."

CW4 Patricia Frances Shaw

First Female to be Commissioned as a Warrant Officer

CW4 Shaw was born June 23, 1946, in Heber Springs, Arkansas. However, she grew up in North Little Rock and graduated from North Little Rock High School in 1965. She attended Arkansas State Teacher's College (now UCA) for two years.

CW4 Shaw enlisted in the Arkansas National Guard on June 21, 1975, as a Private First Class where she was assigned to Det 1, HHD, 39th Support Battalion. She was then transferred to the 936th Aviation Company where she received her commission as a Warrant Officer One, becoming the Unit Personnel Technician on October 18, 1977. Arkansas' first female to be commissioned as a Warrant Officer.

CW4 Shaw was one of the original members of the "Full-time Recruiting and Retention Force." On October 1, 1976, she was placed on one of the first "temporary duty" assignments for a period of one year. This type of "temporary duty" was the birth of the Active Guard/Reserve (AGR) Program. Upon renewal of her temporary orders, she was assigned as the Recruiting and Induction Officer in Headquarters, Arkansas Army National Guard or STARC.

She was reassigned on September 29, 1985, as the Recruiting and Retention Specialist. On January 7, 1991, after more than 15 years in the recruitment area, she was moved to the Department of Personnel and Administration, present day Deputy Chief of Staff, Personnel. She was soon promoted to Chief Warrant Officer Four.

CW4 Shaw was instrumental in planning the first Minuteman Youth Seminar Camp for disadvantaged children in 1987 and continued to volunteer her services until retirement.

She was active in the Boy Scouts of America program for over 15 years. While working with the Boy Scouts, she served on several committees as well as preparing and serving meals for Scout Banquets. She procured staff and supplies for the National Invitational White River Canoe Race which the Arkansas National Guard helped sponsor for many years. She was presented the Boy Scouts of America Silver Beaver Award for her service.

Shaw's decorations and awards include the Meritorious Service Medal, Army Commendation Medal, Army Achievement Medal, Armed Forces Reserve Medal (2nd Award), National Defense Service Medal, Army Reserve Component Achievement Medal (5th Award), Army Service Ribbon (4th Award), Arkansas Recruiting Ribbon, and the National Guard Bureau's Minuteman Award.

CW4 Shaw retired from the Arkansas Army National Guard on June 3, 1996. Retirement did not last long. She became a Kitchen Consultant for The Pampered Chef and worked with the 2000 Census Bureau as Finance Supervisor for the Little Rock Office. She enrolled and completed the H & R Block Income Tax Course. Upon completion of the course, she was a tax consultant for several years. In 2003, she decided it was time to really retire and enjoy her grandchildren, go camping and travel the world.

Lieutenant Colonel
Melissa H. Shipman

First Female Instructor Pilot
Arkansas Army National Guard

First Female Assault Helicopter
Company Commander
C Co 1-185th Air Assault

First Female Brigade Aviation
Officer 39th Infantry Brigade
Combat Team

Lieutenant Colonel (LTC.) Melissa Helaine Shipman, a trailblazing figure in the Arkansas National Guard, has distinguished herself as the first female instructor pilot, first female air assault company commander, and the first female 39th Infantry Brigade Combat Team brigade aviation officer.

A native of Little Rock, Arkansas, LTC Shipman's journey is a testament to her dedication and passion for service. Her journey from a mechanic to an esteemed instructor pilot illustrates a remarkable career trajectory marked by dedication, skill, and determination. LTC Shipman's achievements serve as a beacon of inspiration, particularly for women in the military, proving that with commitment and hard work, barriers can be broken, and new paths forged.

LTC Shipman graduated from Parkview High School in May 1996, and received a Bachelor of Arts in Liberal Studies and Information Technology from the University of Arkansas Little Rock in 2002. LTC Shipman is currently attending the United States Army War College to pursue a master's education in strategic studies.

LTC Shipman joined the Arkansas National Guard in 2002 to pursue a career that embodied service and commitment. She began her tenure in the National Guard as a UH60 Blackhawk Maintainer with the 172nd Aeromedical Evacuation Company, where she gained invaluable experience working on helicopters at the Army Aviation Support Facility. Her attendance at Officer Candidate School marked her transition from enlisted service to an officer. She commissioned as a distinguished honor graduate and Aviation Branch Officer in August 2005.

Key leadership roles and numerous staff assignments mark her post-commission journey. After completing the Aviation Officer Basic Course and flight school, LTC Shipman served in the 1st Battalion 114th Aviation Regiment, "Eagles of Liberty." She has been a flight platoon leader and Commander in Company C, 1-185th Air Assault. She was the first female to command the company in 2011, making her also the first female in the Arkansas Army National Guard to command a company level combat arms unit. She held various positions in the 1st-114th battalion staff, including assistant operations officer and logistics officer. She was deployed to Kosovo for a peacekeeping mission as part of a NATO coalition in 2010, providing stability and aviation support to the local population. Her roles as the Operations Officer (S3), Executive Officer (XO), and Battalion Commander for the 1-114th Security and Support Aviation Regiment, where she was responsible for leading 400 Soldiers and managing an aircraft fleet of 28 helicopters, highlight her exceptional resilience and leadership. In her current role as the 77th Theater Aviation Brigade Executive Officer, LTC Shipman continues to demonstrate her leadership and aviation expertise.

Lieutenant Colonel Shipman's commitment to continual learning is evident in her extensive military education. She has completed several prestigious courses, including the Aviation Captains Career Course, High Altitude Army Aviation Training Site (HAATS) Power Management Course, Instructor Pilot Course, Command and General Staff Officer Course, Advanced Operations Course, Human Resource Management Qualification Course, Support Operations Course, Air Cavalry Leaders Course, Joint Airspace and Operations Command and Control Course, the Air Defense Airspace Management and Brigade Aviation Element Course, the UH-60M Aircraft Qualification Transition, among others. Her qualifications as a UH-60 Helicopter Pilot in Command and Flight Instructor, along with her Senior Army Aviator Badge, underscore her aviation technical prowess. She is the first female to achieve Flight Instructor qualifications and did so in 2012. In 2018 she served as the first female brigade aviation officer in the 39th Infantry Brigade.

LTC Shipman has been recognized throughout her career with numerous military awards and decorations, including the Meritorious Service Medal, Army Commendation Medal, Army Achievement Medal, and the Arkansas Exceptional Service Ribbon. Additionally, she is a recipient of the Molly Pitcher, Order of Saint Michael, Samuel Sharpe Keeper of the Flame, and Catherine Greene awards, reflecting her exceptional contributions to the military community.

LTC Shipman is a member of the National Guard Association for Arkansas and the United States. She is a member of the women's international female aviation organization, the Ninety-Nines, where she serves on the scholarship committee helping future female pilots. She is a National Interscholastic Cycling Association (NICA) mountain bike coach coaching and mentoring students from Mount St. Mary, Catholic, and Central high schools. She resides in Sherwood, Arkansas, with her husband Colonel Bryan Shipman. Melissa is a stepmother to four children and a grandmother to seven grandchildren. Her family life complements her distinguished military career, embodying her commitment to service in uniform and at home.

Colonel Sharon (Sherri) Sims

First Female Director of the Army National Guard Education Support Center

First in the National Guard to serve as President of the Council of College and Military Educators

Colonel (COL) Sharon Sims was born in Malvern, Arkansas. She was an "Army Brat" and graduated high school in Stuttgart, Germany. She earned a Bachelor of Science Degree in Business Management from Henderson State University in Arkadelphia, Arkansas, and a Master of Arts Degree in Management and Leadership from Webster University.

COL Sims joined the Arkansas Army National Guard, May 17, 1983, as a Private First Class in the 39th Infantry Brigade (Separate). She received her commission in June 1985 from the Arkansas Military Academy. She was then assigned as a Second Lieutenant in Company A, 39th Infantry Brigade (Separate), where she was the only female officer at the time in that Company. Her next assignment was with the 455th Transportation Battalion, where she held various assignments, including Headquarters and Headquarters Detachment Commander. While in the 455th, she commanded a Rear Detachment for five weeks during Team Spirit in South Korea, responsible for redeploying the Arkansas Guard's military vehicles used during the exercise.

In 1990, COL Sims moved to Washington D.C., where she served with the Joint National Guard Bureau Strategic Planning Office, and then with the Office of the Secretary of Defense Reserve Affairs. Both assignments were at the Pentagon.

COL Sims went on to serve in a variety of positions in the Arkansas Army National Guard including Assistant Operations Officer and Public Affairs Officer for the National Guard Marksmanship Training Center, S-1 of 87th Troop Command, Secretary to the General Staff (SGS), Soldier Services Branch Chief, and Deputy State Surgeon, Arkansas Medical Command. She culminated her career as the state's G-1 and Strategic Planning Officer.

COL Sims took a five-year hiatus from her full-time military status and served as the first Director/Program Manager for the National Guard Bureau Education Support Center, which was formed in 2002. During this time, she also served on the Executive Board of the Council of Colleges and Military Educators (CCME), culminating in being President of that organization.

COL Sims' professional military education includes Adjutant General Officer Basic Course, Transportation Officer Advance Course, Public Affairs School, Combined Arms Service Support School, Command and General Staff Officer Course, and a variety of training courses in organizational development and strategic planning.

COL Sims' military awards include the Legion of Merit, Meritorious Service Medal (3), Army Commendation Medal (3), Army Achievement Medal, Army Reserve Component Achievement Medal (8), National Defense Service Medal (2), Armed Forces Reserve Medal (2), Air Force Organizational Excellence Award, the Army Service Ribbon, and the Army Reserve Overseas Training Ribbon (6). State awards include the Arkansas Distinguished Service Medal, the Arkansas Exceptional Service Medal (2), and the Arkansas Commendation Medal.

COL Sims retired in 2013, with 29 years and nine months of distinguished military service. She was inducted into the Arkansas National Guard OCS Hall of Fame in October 2018 for her exceptional service. She has been married to Colonel Larry Sims since February 14, 1997. They currently reside on Table Rock Lake in Hollister, Missouri.

Colonel Sara A. Stigler

First Female Deputy Commander of 188th Wing

First Female Commander of 188th Intelligence, Surveillance and Reconnaissance Group

First Commander and Female Commander 153rd Intelligence Squadron

Colonel (Col.) Sara A. Stigler was born and raised in Texas. She graduated from Caldwell High School. Col. Stigler was inspired to serve in the military as a young child, having been raised in a military family. Her maternal grandfather served as a U.S. Navy Aviator and her paternal grandfather served as a U.S. Air Force Medical Physician. Col. Stigler had the opportunity to tour the USAF Academy at the young age of seven. She knew she would attend the Academy as soon as she saw the campus. Col. Stigler aligned her academic and extra-curricular goals with her dream to attend the Academy to ensure acceptance. She was accepted into the USAF Academy and earned her Bachelor of Science in History in May 2000.

Upon graduation from the USAF Academy, Col. Stigler was selected to become an Intelligence Officer and served in the USAF from 2000-2007. During her active-duty career, Col. Stigler enjoyed many assignments. She has deployed overseas in support of contingencies Enduring Freedom and Iraqi Freedom, in which she was by-named to forward deploy in support of the 82nd Airborne Division providing time-critical intelligence to tactical airlift operations. She has fond memories of her active-duty career. Her most endearing times were her assignment at Pope AFB, North

Carolina, Osan Air Base in the Republic of Korea, and her deployment in support of Iraqi Freedom attached to the 82nd Airborne Division.

In 2010, Col. Stigler joined the Arkansas Air National Guard as Chief, Wing Intelligence at the 188th Operations Group, 188th Wing in Fort Smith. During her time with the 188th Operations Group, she was selected to deploy with the wing's A-10C aircraft to Afghanistan in support of Operation Enduring Freedom. In 2014, The 188th Fighter Wing underwent a major mission conversion transitioning from the manned A-10C aircraft to multiple mission sets including Intelligence, Surveillance and Reconnaissance (ISR). Col. Stigler was hand selected to create, develop, and ready the 153rd Intelligence Squadron, garnering her recognition for not only becoming the first female Commander, but also the first ever Commander of that squadron. Her knowledge and leadership provided the squadron with the necessary stability required to become fully mission capable in short order. Col. Stigler then commanded the 123rd Intelligence Squadron from March 2017 – April 2018, before she was selected to become the first female 188th ISR Group Commander. She held that position from April 2018 – September 2021, when she was selected to serve as the first female 188th Vice Wing Commander. She continues to serve in that role, and her duty title became 188th Wing Deputy Commander in August 2023 again being the first female in this role.

Although she never set out to do so, Col. Stigler has become a pioneer in many ways through the course of her service in the Arkansas Guard and has inspired many women to follow her though the trail she has blazed.

In November 2022, Col. Stigler's spouse was selected to serve as the 189th Airlift Wing Commander, Little Rock AFB. His selection subsequently brought about another title for Col. Stigler, she is the first actively serving spouse to the 189th Airlift Wing Commander.

During her downtime, Col. Stigler enjoys hiking, camping, and other outdoor activities. Col. Stigler is a loving mother of two and spends most of her free time with her husband, children and friends participating in outdoor recreation.

SGT Nancy Stokes

First Female in Kuwait During the Operation Desert Storm Ground War

SGT Stokes was born on August 17, 1958, and raised in Arkansas graduating from Rogers High School in 1976. SGT Stokes enlisted in the Arkansas Army National Guard on August 31, 1987. She was assigned to Headquarters and Headquarters Battery, 142nd Field Artillery Brigade. She attended U.S. Army Basic Training in Fort Jackson, South Carolina followed by Advanced Individual Training (AIT) at Fort Gordon, South Carolina. She graduated from AIT on March 18, 1988, with a Military Occupational Specialty of 31C10, Single Channel Radio Operator.

She was activated with the 142nd FA Brigade on September 20, 1990, for service in Saudi Arabia during Operation Desert Storm/Desert Shield. SGT Stokes was the first female in Kuwait during the ground war of Operation Desert Storm. She served with the HHB 142nd FA BDE as Radio Repair/GPS Installer. The unit served overseas from November 21, 1990, until their active-duty deployment ended on June 5, 1991.

SGT Stokes held many nontraditional positions for females during her early career. She was a Rogers Police Department Radio operator and civilian law-enforcement officer for the Bentonville Police Department and Ozark Security Patrol Supervisor between 1976 and 1980. She was an equipment operator for Scott Paper Company from 1981 through 1984. From 1985 to 1987, she worked for Rockwell International building parts and advanced composites for the Space Shuttle.

She began a position as a U.S. Postal Service letter carrier in 1993.

Her military education includes the Primary Leadership Development Course (PLDC) and Basic Noncommissioned Officer Course (BNCOC). She was awarded two additional Military Occupational Specialties; the 31U20, Communications Maintenance and 63R20, Light Wheeled Vehicle Mechanic.

SGT Stoke's service was recognized for its excellence through the receipt of the following awards, decorations, and honors to include the Bronze Star, Army Achievement Medal, Army Reserve Components Achievement Medal, National Defense Medal, Army Service Ribbon, Southwest Asia Campaign Ribbon with 3 Bronze Stars, the Kuwait Liberation Medal (Saudi Arabia), the Kuwait Liberation Medal (Kuwait), and Army Reserve Component Training Ribbon.

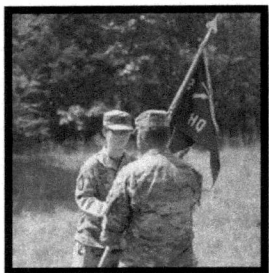

Major Megan E. Thomas

Frist Female to Graduate from Maneuver Captains Career Course (MCCC), serve as an Infantry Line Company Commander, and Infantry Battalion Operations Officer, Arkansas Army National Guard

Major (MAJ) Megan Elizabeth Thomas was born September 1, 1986, in Hot Springs, Arkansas, and graduated from Ouachita High School in 2004. MAJ Thomas earned a Bachelor's Degree in Secondary Education with a major in Physical Education and a minor in Health from Henderson State University in 2009. MAJ Thomas also earned a Master's Degree in Executive Leadership from Liberty University in 2021.

MAJ Thomas enlisted into the Arkansas Army National Guard on February 25, 2005, as a Multi-Transmissions Systems Operator and Maintainer (25Q). She was mobilized in October 2005 to support the humanitarian relief efforts in Louisiana following the destruction caused by Hurricane Katrina. In 2006, she attended and graduated from the Army Airborne School. In December 2009, she commissioned into the Arkansas Army National Guard through the Henderson State University ROTC program as a Medical Service Officer (70B).

Her first assignment was a Medivac Platoon Leader with the 296th Medical Company. In 2012, she chose to branch transfer to a Military Police Officer (31A) to prepare for the upcoming deployment to Afghanistan. In July 2014, she deployed to Afghanistan with the 216th Military Police Company as the Company Operations Officer. She took command of the 216th Military Police Company in March 2015, after returning home from the unit's deployment.

MAJ Thomas was the first female in the Arkansas Army National Guard to graduate Maneuver Captains Career Course (MCCC), serve as an Infantry Line Company Commander, and Infantry Battalion Operations Officer. Major Thomas graduated from MCCC in January 2019. She served as an Officer Candidate School TAC Officer from July 2017 to August 2019. She took command of HHC 2-153rd IN from August 2019 to September 2020. MAJ Thomas served as the Plans Officer for the 39th Infantry Brigade Combat Team from September 2020 to June 2021, followed by a successful command of Bravo Company 2-153rd IN from July 2021 to August 2022.

MAJ Thomas is the Battalion Operations officer (S3) for Task Force Gunslinger, 2-153rd IN (deployed). The unit was headquartered at Prince Sultan Air Force Base (PSAB), Kingdom of Saudi Arabia. She has designed both Security Force operations and theater security cooperation training exercises across the Kingdom of Saudi Arabia, Jordan, United Arab Emirates, Qatar, Kuwait, Kazakhstan, Iran, and Israel. TF Gunslinger staff was selected to participate in a Division Level exercise with the Israeli Defense Forces

Throughout her military career she has dedicated time to serve and support the Gold Star Families of Arkansas. Since 2008, she has volunteered her time to serve on the Military Funeral Honors team, rendering final honors to over 300 Service Members, Retirees, and Veterans throughout the State of Arkansas.

Significant Experiences (Infantry): HHC 2-153rd IN, Commander - Task Force Commander (100 Infantry Soldiers) during the 2020 Civil Disturbance State Active-Duty mission in Arkansas. B Co. 2-153rd IN, Commander – successfully led Soldiers through a Combined Training Center (CTC) Rotation 2021 at the Joint Readiness Training Center and two Live Fire Exercise (LFX) validations (one platoon and one company) Observer/Controller (OCT) for Joint Readiness Training Center, Brigade S3 2-153rd IN, S3/Operations Officer – Deployed with Task Force Gunslinger in support of Operation Spartan Shield 2023.

**Staff Seargent
Chloe M. Thompson**

**First Female Enlisted
Field Artillery Soldier**

Staff Sergeant (SSG) Chloe M. Thompson was born in Little Rock, Arkansas, and graduated from Cabot High School in 2018. She is enrolled in the Bachelor of Science in Business Administration in Business Analytics degree program at Arkansas State University.

SSG Chloe Thompson enlisted in the Arkansas Army National Guard on April 3, 2018, as a 13B, a cannon crew member. Since her enlistment, she has been a member of Charlie Battery 1/206th conducting the different positions within the section.

On February 1, 2019, SSG Chloe Thompson completed 13B, Cannon Crewmember, Military Occupation Specialty (MOS) School, becoming the first female enlisted field artillery Soldier in the Arkansas National Guard. She became a member of Charlie Battery 1/206th on April 12, 2019, and progressed to the role of M777A2 Section Chief. SSG Chloe Thompson was awarded the Honorable Order of Saint Barbara on June 16, 2023. She finishes her first 6-year service obligation with the Arkansas Army National Guard on April 3, 2024, and looks forward to many years ahead of her.

SSG Thompson completed Basic Combat Training on November 20, 2019, Duty MOS qualification on February 1, 2019, Basic Leader Course on September 25, 2020, Advanced Leader Course on November 22, 2022, and United Movement Officer Course on April 10, 2021.

SSG Thompson's awards include the Army Achievement Medal and the Army Commendation Medal.

Beyond military commitments, SSG Thompson finds fulfillment in spending time with her family, reading, and running.

Major Robin (Lowery) Tolliver

First Female Troop Medical Clinic Commander

First Winter Biathlon Coordinator/Participant for Arkansas

First Female Physician Assistant and Aeronautical Physician Assistant for Arkansas Army National Guard

Major (MAJ) Tolliver was born in Bastrop, Louisiana. She graduated from Crossett High School in 1987. MAJ Tolliver began her military career in the Arkansas Army National Guard immediately after graduation in June 1987 with the 216th Medical Company as a combat medic. She began working at the Arkansas Military Academy for a course called Battleskills, which she later also graduated as a student. She later transferred to the 148th Evacuation Hospital while attending training for Licensed Practical Nursing at Oil Belt Vocational Technical School in Eldorado. She graduated as valedictorian of her class in 1990. In 1994, she completed her Associate of Applied Science in Nursing as a Registered Nurse (RN) from Arkansas State University–Beebe. She then worked in a civilian emergency department and joined the 172nd Medevac as a flight medic. She served as the Air Ambulance Platoon Sergeant and achieved the rank of Sergeant First Class (SFC/E-7). During this time, she completed PLDC, BNCOC, and ANCOC.

She coordinated Arkansas' first winter biathlon team, which involved skiing and shooting. She established a team and was the only participating female for 2 years in both Minnesota and Vermont. From 1999 to 2001, she attended the Interservice

Physician Assistant Program at Fort Sam Houston in San Antonio, Texas, where she obtained her Bachelor of Science Degree in Physician Assistant (PA) studies. After graduating PA school, she received her commission as a Second Lieutenant and was relocated to the 205th Medical Co. She completed her Master's Degree in Physician Assistant Studies with a specialty in Emergency Medicine through the University of Nebraska in 2003.

In 2004, she voluntarily joined the 39th Infantry Brigade for an 18-month deployment to Iraq as a First Lieutenant. She served as the only female medical provider and female crisis advocate. She participated in routine and emergent treatment of soldiers and prisoners and was part of numerous precarious missions that included medical capabilities/treatment to surrounding villages, bringing supplies to orphanages, late night combat missions, relocating downtown to a smaller area of Baghdad when there was a break in their providers, and joining the 2/7 Cavalry in Najaf during combat operations to provide medical care to civilian casualties. She was present to witness some of the brigade's most difficult days treating combat casualties from mortar fire within her own battalion, for which she received the Bronze Star. Upon returning home, she remained on active duty as a Captain at the Troop Medical Clinic on Camp Robinson as a Physician Assistant. She became a strong advocate for soldiers experiencing Post Traumatic Stress after returning home. She eventually became the first female commander of the clinic in 2006. MAJ Tolliver was the distinguished honor graduate for the Army Flight Surgeon course in 2006 at Fort Rucker, Alabama, which allowed her to simultaneously serve as an Aeronautical Physician Assistant for the 1/114th Aviation and Troop Medical Clinic Commander until she retired in 2010 with 22 years of service.

MAJ Tolliver's awards and decorations includes Bronze Star, Meritorious Service Medal (2nd award), Army Commendation Medal (6th award), Army Achievement Medal (5th award), Joint

Meritorious Unit Award, Army Reserve Component Achievement Medal (6th award), National Defense Service Medal (2nd award), Global War on Terrorism Expeditionary Medal, Humanitarian Service Medal, Noncommissioned Officer Professional Development Ribbon (3rd award), Army Service Ribbon, Overseas Service Ribbon, Armed Forces Reserve Medal w/M Device (2nd award), Combat Medical Badge, Arkansas Distinguished Service Medal, ARK Federal Service ribbon (2nd award), ARK Emergency Service Ribbon (2nd award), Arkansas Service Ribbon (2nd award), Louisiana Emergency Service medal.

Command Sergeant Major
Tammy J. Treat

First Female First Sergeant for 119th Mobile Public Affairs Detachment

First Female Command Sergeant Major for 871st Troop Command Battalion Arkansas Army National Guard

Command Sergeant Major (CSM) Tammy Treat was born November 10, 1973, in Norwood, Massachusetts. She was the daughter of a sailor and grew up on several DOD installations. She is a 1992 graduate of Cotter High School, holds an Associate of Science, Vincennes University, and a Bachelor of Social Work, Appalachian State University.

On May 2, 1991, during her junior year in Cotter High School, CSM Treat enlisted via the split option program. At the age of seventeen, she attended basic combat training at Fort Leonard Wood, Missouri, returned home and began her career in the 224th (-) Maintenance Company. After graduating high school in March 1992, she attended Advance Individual Training (AIT) at Fort Benjamin Harrison, Indiana. She earned her first MOS of 75B, Personnel Administrative Specialist. CSM Treat earned her second MOS of 92A, Automated Logistical Specialist in May 1995. During CSM Treat's years with the 224th, she had several overseas annual trainings including Italy and Germany.

In March 2003, CSM Treat was ordered to active service at Fort Sill, Oklahoma with the 224th Maintenance Company in support of Operation Enduring Freedom. Her deployment concluded in October 2003, and she was assigned to the 217th Brigade Support Battalion as a Material Management Supervisor. After returning from Fort Sill, CSM

Treat became a SARRS-1 instructor for the Professional Education Center at Camp Robinson.

In 2007, CSM Treat moved to North Carolina to be with her family, only to receive notification to report for pre-mobilization physical for Operation Iraq Freedom. She was assigned to the 39th Infantry Brigade Combat Team to work with the 1-151st Cavalry Squadron, C Troop, to complete pre-mobilization exercises at C Troop's home station and Fort Chaffee.

On December 20, 2007, CSM Treat received orders to report to the 216th Military Police by January 5, 2008, to complete pre-mobilization training at Camp Shelby, Mississippi. CSM Treat was assigned to the 216th MP Co as a cook as documented on her DD214 for her service in Iraq. However, this was not her actual assignment or actual duties. She was with the 39th IBCT, C Squadron, 1-151st Cav. She served as Tactical Operations Supervisor while also going on missions as a gunner or a truck commander while performing logistical convoy escort missions. CSM Treat spent her rare downtime moonlighting as a journalist and volunteering at a children's burn clinic in Scania Iraq. She treated burn wounds of those turned away from local hospitals, resulting in her receiving her most prized award, the Military Outstanding Volunteer Service Medal (MOVSM). Proof of this assignment is documented within The Army Driver – W Badge, Award of the Golden Spurs, MOVSM, and the Army Commendation Medal. CSM Treat was released from active duty and assigned to 119th Public Mobile Affairs on January 30, 2009. CSM Treat was promoted to First Sergeant of the 119th Public Mobile Affairs Unit in 2009 or 2010 being the first female 1SG for the unit. In 2012 she was reassigned to the 87th Troop Command Battalion as the acting Command Sergeant Major.

CSM Treat was promoted to the rank of Command Sergeant Major on April 1, 2013, and was assigned as the CSM for the 871st Troop Command Battalion, being first Female CSM for this battalion and the third CSM in the state. In 2016 CSM Treat served as the Task Force

CSM and senior enlisted advisor to the Task Force Red Wolf Beyond the Horizon commander in Guatemala.

After 25 years of service, many flights and road trips from North Carolina to Arkansas, CSM Treat retired on August 1, 2016. Her awards and decorations include: Legion of Merit, Army Commendation Medal (2), Army Achievement Medal (3); Army Good Conduct Medal, Army Reserve Component Achievement Medal (5), National Defense Service Medal (2), Iraq Campaign Medal, Global War on Terrorism Service Medal, Armed Forces Service Medal, Military Outstanding Volunteer Service Medal, Armed Forces Reserve Medal with "M" Device (2), Overseas Service Ribbon, Army Reserve Component Overseas Training Ribbon (2), Arkansas Federal Service Ribbon (2), Arkansas Service Ribbon (3), the Army Driver-W Badge and the Order of the Golden Spur.

She now resides in Wilkesboro, North Carolina. Upon retirement, CSM Treat started volunteering in her community. She is a certified court appointed special advocate for children in the care of child protective services. She has held fundraisers to assist in feeding the needy, provide funding for dog rescue organizations, and a residential childcare facility. In 2022 she earned her Bachelor's Degree in Social Work and currently works for a local non-profit as a Justice Liaison and Peer Guide. She assists those in or being released from local jails and prisons, advocating for treatment and resources to assist participants reentering their communities. She is also an advisor for her county's newly formed crisis intervention team.

**Sergeant Major
Donna Ivey Walker**

**First Female Directorate of Personnel
Sergeant Major
Arkansas Army National Guard**

Sergeant Major (SGM) Donna Ivey Walker was born in Russellville, Arkansas and spent her childhood and youth in Danville where she graduated from Danville High School in 1973. After attending Arkansas Tech University for two years, she worked at the Arkansas River Valley Regional Library until she enlisted in the Arkansas Army National Guard.

SGM Walker began her military career on January 16, 1978, enlisting in the 439th Signal Platoon, Little Rock. After Basic and Advanced Individual Training, she served as a Personnel Records Specials until she transferred to STARC (-) AR ARNG State Headquarters where she served as a Production Recruiter until 1980. While assigned to STARC, she worked as a Senior Pay Specialist at the United States Property and Fiscal Office at Camp Robinson until 1984 when she was assigned to the Department of Personnel where she served as a Personnel Information Systems Training Noncommissioned Officer (NCO). During this time, Walker was designated an honor graduate at the Basic NCO Course at Camp Robinson. She also served on the Governors Color Guard and in 1987, she had the distinct honor of being selected to represent the Arkansas Army National Guard in the Fifth U. S. Army FORSCOM Soldier and NCO of the Year competition. In 1989, she became the Personnel Sergeant for the Retirement Points Accounting System and in 1990, she was assigned to National Guard Bureau, Professional Education Center, where she served as an instructor. While being assigned to NGB, she also served as a Force

Development Staff NCO in Arlington, Virginia. After completing the United Sergeants Major Academy in Fort Bliss, Texas in 1994, SGM Walker was transferred back to State Headquarters, Camp Robinson where she served as NCOIC for the Personnel Services Branch and then became the Senior Personnel Supervisor for the Directorate of Personnel in 1995. On September 3, 1999, she had the honor of being the first female to be promoted to Sergeant Major for the Directorate of Personnel. SGM Walker served in this capacity until her retirement on March 31, 2001, with 23 years of service.

SGM Walker and her husband CSM (Ret) Romie Walker, live in Cabot, where they have enjoyed gardening and camping during their retirement. SGM Walker graduated from Central Arkansas Bible College (CABC) in Jacksonville, where she received a Doctor of Theology in 2013. She has served CABC in an administrative support capacity for several years. In 2015, she received her Certificate of Ordination through Word Churches International.

Sergeant First Class
Tasheenia L. Wallace

First Female to Graduate From the 11B Infantry Transition Course, Arkansas Army National Guard

Sergeant First Class (SFC) Tasheenia Wallace was born in Denver, Colorado. She grew up in Morrilton, Arkansas and graduated from Wonderview High School in 2004. She received a Bachelor's Degree in Business Administration in 2015 from Philander Smith College in Little Rock, Arkansas, and she is currently working on her Master's Degree in Human Resources and Leadership, and she is scheduled to graduate in May of 2024.

SFC Wallace joined the Arkansas Army National Guard in 2004, after graduating high school, but had a break in service until 2006, where she then attended Basic Training and Advanced Individual Training at Fort Leonard Wood, Missouri. She started her Army career as a Chemical Specialist (74D) at Headquarters and Headquarters Company, 39th Brigade Special Troops Battalion. In 2007, she started her premobilization for the 2008-2009 Iraqi Freedom Deployment with the 2nd Battalion 153rd Infantry, 39th Infantry Brigade.

In 2010, SFC Wallace was hired to work full-time in the Active/Guard and Reserve (AGR) Program as an NBC Team Member for the 61st Civil Support Team (WMD) at Camp J.T. Robinson, North Little Rock, Arkansas. She was later promoted CBRN Noncommissioned Officer (NCO) and Team Chief on the Survey Team. In 2015, SFC Wallace transferred to the 1-151st Calvary Squadron as the Human Resources Sergeant. As the results of 1-151st Calvary Squadron deactivation, she was transferred to 1st Battalion 153rd Infantry and served as the Human Resources Sergeant.

In 2017, SFC Wallace made history for the Arkansas National Guard when she became the first female to graduate from the 11B, Infantry Transition Course (ITC), at the Robinson Maneuver Training Center. In 2018 SFC Wallace was promoted to Sergeant First Class and then assigned to Company B, 1-153rd Infantry Battalion, Texarkana, AR as a Platoon Sergeant during the training at the Joint Readiness Training Center, Fort Polk, Louisiana. In 2021, She was reassigned to Headquarters and Headquarters Company (HHC, Det 1), 1st Battalion, 153rd Infantry as an Assistant Operations NCO. Later in 2021, SFC Wallace was assigned to the 61st Civil Support Team (WMD) as an Operations NCO. In 2022, she was assigned to 2nd Battalion, 233rd Regional Training Institute (RTI) as a Senior Instructor Writer where she is currently serving.

SFC Wallace's military courses includes the Advanced Leader Common Core Course, ARNG Basic Human Resources and Admin Course, Human Resources Senior Leaders Course Phase I, Human Resources Senior Leaders Course Phase II, Master Leader's Course, 11B Infantry Transition Course and Retirement Services Training.

For her outstanding service, SFC Wallace has received the following medals and awards: Meritorious Service Medal, Army Commendation Medal, Army Achievement Medal, National Defense Service Medal, Noncommissioned Officer Professional Development Ribbon, Army Service Ribbon, Overseas Service Ribbon, Driver Mechanic Badge/Driver Wheeled Vehicle Badge, Armed Forces Reserve Medal, Global War on Terrorism Medal, Afghanistan Campaign Medal, Arkansas National Guard Service Ribbon, Arkansas National Guard Federal Service Ribbon, Arkansas National Guard Service Ribbon, and the COL Robert L. Manning Achievement Medal.

Lieutenant Colonel
Joyce Wilkerson

First Enlisted Female in the
Arkansas Air National Guard

First Female Squadron Commander in the
189th Tactical Airlift Group (TAG)

Lieutenant Colonel (Lt. Col.) Joyce Wilkerson was the first enlisted female in the Arkansas Air National Guard, and the seventh in the nation, enlisting in August 1969. After serving for eleven and a half years as an enlisted member, she was commissioned in 1981. She served in several capacities in the 189th Tactical Airlift Group (TAG). She was the first female to be appointed Squadron Commander in the Arkansas Air National Guard. Later she became the Commander of the 189th Mission Support Squadron

In her civilian capacity with the 189th TAG, Lt. Col. Wilkerson serves as Military Personnel Management Officer.

Information obtained from *Patchwork of Our Lives Women's Recognition Day 1992*

Chief Master Sergeant
Donna Lynn Witherow

First Female Chief Master Sergeant
189th Airlift Wing
Arkansas Air National Guard

Chief Master Sergeant (CMSgt) Donna Lynn Witherow was born in Cleveland, Ohio and raised in Chardon, a small town north of Cleveland. She and her twin sister were in foster care until the age of three months. They were adopted by good Christian parents. CMSgt Witherow is grateful for the adoption of herself and her sister. She said, "It was truly a blessing."

CMSgt Witherow's father served in the Army Air Corps, and from a young age she became in awe of him and his travels, hence, the beginning of her love for the military. In her junior year of high school, she decided to join the Air Force during the Vietnam Era. After graduating high school in Chardon, Ohio, in May 1973, two months later, she enlisted in the United States Air Force on July 5, 1973.

CMSgt Witherow joined the Air Force when women were called Women in the Air Force (WAFs). She said, "WAFs had their own dorms and squadrons; they were kept a good distance from the males." Chief Witherow's recruiter initially indicated that she would be in the medical career field upon completion of Air Force Basic Training at San Antonio, Texas. She later learned that she would be assigned to a maintenance career field. She graduated from technical school at Sheppard AFB, Texas and served as a C-130 (43131F) Crew Chief at Little Rock AFB, Arkansas.

There were six females assigned to the 314th Organizational Maintenance Squadron (OMS), Little Rock AFB. At that time, the Air Force began assigning females to male jobs for equal opportunity purposes. The 314th OMS Squadron was in absolute shock when the women arrived! They were not prepared for them as there were no bathroom facilities for the females. They eventually made do by hanging a sign on the door in the hangar specifying female facilities. Special rules existed for women. Some rules indicated that women could not work at night nor work with any single male crew chiefs. Though there were ups and downs, joining the military was a great experience for Chief Witherow. On June 11, 1976, CMSgt Witherow happily accepted an early out due to the United States Air Force Strength Reduction program. She was discharged from active-duty Air Force on the same day.

CMSgt Witherow used her GI Bill to attend a License Practical Nursing (LPN) School and received her LPN license on December 4, 1974. Four years later, she joined the Arkansas Air National Guard as a traditional guardsman at Little Rock AFB. She served in a Medical Service Technician role until she was selected for an Active Guard Reserve (AGR) position as an Association Health Technician in the 189th Medical Squadron in 1981. Chief Witherow also held positions at Andrew AFB, Washington D.C., and the Air National Guard Readiness Center. In 1991, during Desert Storm, she deployed to Nocton Hall, England to help set up a 750-bed contingency hospital.

Chief Witherow was promoted to Chief Master Sergeant on August 3, 1996, and became the first female to achieve this rank in the Arkansas Air National Guard. She retired as an Active Guard Reservist on April 1, 2005.

CMSgt Witherow's awards and decorations include, but are not limited to, the Air Force Achievement Medal, Air Force Commendation Medal with two devices, Meritorious Service Medal, and the National Defense Service Medal with two devices.

Since retirement, CMSgt Witherow enjoys traveling with her husband in their motorhome. She also enjoys serving in her church, fishing, reading, and gardening. She is blessed to share retirement with her husband Barry, three children, two bonus children, fourteen grandchildren, and two great-grandchildren.

Colonel Charlotte Yates

First Female Author of the Arkansas Army National Guard Field Sanitation Manual

Colonel (COL) Yates was the Arkansas State Chief Nurse.

In civilian life, COL Yates is Health and Nursing Services Specialist for the Arkansas Department of Education, where she was in charge of the nursing services for all the school districts in the state. COL Yates received a Master's Degree in Education and in 1992 was pursuing a post-graduate degree.

COL Yates taught CPR classes and lead discussions on health careers and other health related subjects on television and radio. COL Yates is the author of the *Field Sanitation Manual* used by the Arkansas Army National Guard.

Information obtained from *Patchwork of Our Lives Women's Recognition Day 1992*

Lieutenant Colonel
Sandra Y. Young

**First Female Commander
217th Brigade Support Battalion,
142nd Field Artillery Brigade
Arkansas Army National Guard**

Lieutenant Colonel (LTC) Sandra Y. Young is a native of Dermott, Arkansas. She graduated from Dermott High School in 1993. Upon graduation, LTC Young attended the University of Arkansas at Little Rock. In 2004, she completed her Bachelor of Science in Organizational Management from Nyack College, New York, and her Master of Science in Emergency Disaster Management from Trident University.

LTC Young began her outstanding military career in the Arkansas National Guard on July 15, 1992. She attended basic training in Fort Jackson, South Carolina, and advanced individual training in Fort Gordon, Georgia, where she graduated from the Signal Corps as a Signal Support System Specialist (31U). LTC Young's enlisted career started in the 1122nd Transportation Company, Monticello, Arkansas, 205th Medical Support Company, Lake Village, Arkansas, and Company C, 212th Signal Battalion, Pine Bluff, Arkansas.

LTC Young received her officer commission from the Arkansas National Guard, 233rd Regional Training Institute's Officer Candidate School on August 19, 2000. Upon commissioning, she was assigned to the 1123rd Transportation Company in Marked Tree, Arkansas. LTC Young attended her Officer Basic Course in Fort Eustis, Virginia, where she graduated from the Transportation Corps on March 2, 2001. She was assigned to the Washington, D.C. National Guard as a Transportation Officer Platoon Leader with the 140th Transportation Company on May 8, 2001. Her additional assignments included:

Executive Officer, 140th Transportation Company; Company Commander, 140th Transportation Company; Company Commander, 547th Transportation; International Affairs Officer, J5/J7; S1, 74th Troop Command; Secretary, General Staff, Headquarters-District of Columbia; G4 Plans and Policy Officer, Headquarters-District of Columbia ARNG; G4, Operations Officers, U.S. Army Central Command; Deputy G4, Headquarters- District of Columbia National Guard; G4 Senior Logistics Staff Officer, National Guard Bureau and Deputy G4, Joint Force Headquarters-Arkansas, Camp J.T. Robinson.

On August 20, 2020, LTC Young was selected as the Battalion Commander, 217th Brigade Support Battalion, 142nd Field Artillery Brigade, Arkansas Army National Guard. She was the first female assigned as a Battalion Commander in the history of the 142nd Field Artillery Brigade. LTC Young has deployed to Jamaica to support U.S. Southern Command and Kuwait/Jordan in support of U.S. Army Central Command.

Her professional military education includes the Transportation Officer Advance Course (2003), Combined Armed Exercise Course (2007), IMCOM-Lean Six Sigma Green Belt (2007), Human Resource Management Qualification Course (2009); Intermediate Level Education (2014); Advanced Operation Course (2017); and How the Army Run Course (2018).

LTC Young's military awards include the Army Superior Unit Award (2nd Award), Meritorious Service Medal (4th Award), Army Commendation Award (4th Award), United States Air Force Commendation (2nd Award), Army Achievement Medal (2nd Award), Air Force Achievement Medal (2nd Award), Army Reserve Component Achievement (4th Award), National Defense Service Medal, Global War on Terrorism Expeditionary Medal, Global War on Terrorism Service Medal, Army Service Ribbon (2nd Award), Armed Forces Reserve Medal (2nd Award/with M Device), U.S. ARCENT Combat Badge, and Army Staff Identification Badge. LTC Young received the Arkansas Officer Candidate School (Class 43) Graduate Leadership

Award and the 87th Troop Command Academic and Leadership Award. She was awarded the District of Columbia National Guard Major General Charles Southward Leadership Award.

One of LTC Young's highest achievements was when she was selected to be the first United States Army Soldier to attend the Caribbean Junior Staff and Command Course, where she successfully graduated on December 9, 2004, in New Castle, Jamaica. LTC Young has been recognized as the only United States Army African American Soldier to complete the international staff course under the Canada National Defense Training Center.

LTC Young is a member of the National Guard Association of the United States. Currently, she supports the Urban League for the State of Arkansas as she assists with providing resources for economic and social development. Her new journey as the President and Chief Executive Officer of RCY Professional and Management Training, Incorporated, allows her to share her military leadership experience with others.

LTC Sandra Young retired on April 30, 2023, after completing over 30 years in the Army National Guard and 22 years of Active Federal Service. LTC Young and her family now reside in Benton, Arkansas.

Colonel Misty Zelk

**First Female Medical Group
Commander, 188th Wing
Arkansas Air National Guard**

Colonel (Col.) Misty Zelk graduated from Twin Lakes Christian School in Mountain Home, Arkansas, in 1987. She attended Evangel University earning a degree in Biology. She commissioned on September 16, 1995, as a senior medical student at the University of Arkansas Medical Sciences and joined the Arkansas Army National Guard as a Second Lieutenant.

Upon graduation, Col. Zelk completed a residency in both internal medicine and pediatrics. During this time, she served with Detachment 4 Med at Camp Joseph T. Robinson, Arkansas. She achieved board certification in both specialties and started private practice in Little Rock. She deployed in 2005 with the 39th Infantry Brigade in support of Operation Iraqi Freedom in Baghdad and Balad, Iraq. Col. Zelk has participated in various humanitarian efforts including Hurricane Katrina with the Arkansas Army National Guard, serving the Joint Task Force along with the 188th Fighter Wing. This experience served as the impetus for her transfer to the Arkansas Air National Guard in 2006. Serving with the 189th Airlift Wing, she participated in the medical training exercise in Guatemala in 2009 and Operation Arctic Care in 2010.

In 2013, Col. Zelk transferred to the 188th Wing where she assumed command as the 188th Medical Group commander during the transition from an A-10 Fighter Wing to the MQ-9 Reaper, Intelligence, Surveillance, Reconnaissance and Targeting Wing. In January 2014, she was promoted to Colonel, becoming the first female Colonel at the

188th Wing and the first female Medical Group commander in the state of Arkansas.

Col. Zelk retired from the Arkansas Air National Guard in December of 2017. She is currently the Medical Director for The Best Defense Foundation, a non-profit organization that returns veterans to their battlefields. The organization currently serves WWII veterans in their return to Normandy for D-Day celebrations, along with commemorations in Germany, Belgium, Amsterdam, and Pearl Harbor along with programs for Korea and future programs for Vietnam.

Conclusion

In 1787, 55 delegates met in Philadelphia, and drafted one of the most significant documents in United States history: The Constitution of the United States. But out of all the signatures on the Constitution, not one belonged to a woman. It was the late Supreme Court Justice Ruth Bader Ginsburg who stated, "Women belong in all places where decisions are being made" (Rajashekara, 2020). And yet, for so long, women were not offered a seat at the tables where such vital decisions were decided.

From the beginning, women have always played instrumental roles in the development and growth of the United States. During the American Revolution, women—such as Deborah Sampson—disguised themselves as men and took up arms against the British to help fight for and secure America's independence. In every U.S. conflict since then, women have served in various capacities, as spies and nurses during the American Civil War; as truck drivers, radio operators, and postal clerks in the Women's Army Corps during World War II; and as combat pilots and infantry soldiers during the Global War on Terrorism.

The dedication to service that we have seen from women throughout our country's history is the same dedication that we continue to witness from female servicemembers in the Arkansas National Guard today. In 1956, women were allowed to join the National Guard as medical officers and in 1968 as enlisted members. Women faced many disparities and limited opportunities, but their determination to excel has been conspicuous, and their impact on the organization is indelible.

Women currently make up 21.4% of the National Guard force nationwide, and this percentage continues to grow (Department of Defense, 2022). The first women who entered the Arkansas National Guard set the foundation and paved the way for many others who would join after them, overcoming obstacles that once seemed insurmountable; and today, many glass ceilings have been broken. The Arkansas National Guard has seen women serving at the highest levels, to include Brigade and Wing Commanders, State Command Sergeant Major, Command Chief Warrant Officer, and General Officers. Lest we forget the various challenges many women had to face, what it took to achieve these accomplishments should never be taken for granted. The stories of women progress and achievement in the Arkansas National Guard will be continuously written. With more progress and more achievements, we will continue to see more women "in all places where decisions are being made."

References

Rajashekara, H. (2020, November 25). Women belong in all places where decisions are being made. https://apolitical.co/solution-articles/en/women-belong-in-all-places-where-decisions-are-being-made

U.S. Department of Defense. (2022, December 14). Department of Defense releases annual demographics report – upward trend in number of women serving continues. U.S. Department of Defense. https://www.defense.gov/News/Releases/Release/Article/3246268/department-of-defense-releases-annual-demographics-report-upward-trend-in-numbe/

www.ingramcontent.com/pod-product-compliance
Lightning Source LLC
Chambersburg PA
CBHW052001090426
42741CB00008B/1487